Obey one, communicate yours and respect all

The Quranic religious policy in a globalised world

Obey one, communicate yours and respect all

The Quranic religious policy in a globalised world

by

Dr. Syed Shahid Ali

Associate Professor
Department of Islamic Studies
Jamia Millia Islamia (central university)

Vij Books India Pvt Ltd
New Delhi (India)

Published by

Vij Books India Pvt Ltd
(Publishers, Distributors & Importers)
2/19, Ansari Road
Delhi – 110 002
Phones: 91-11-43596460, 91-11-47340674
Fax: 91-11-47340674
e-mail: vijbooks@rediffmail.com

Copyright © 2014, *Shahid Ali*

ISBN: 978-93-82652-73-1

Price in India: ₹ 395/-

Contents

Obey one, communicate yours and respect all

In the name of Allah
the Most Gracious, the Most Merciful

Acknowledgements

"One who is not grateful to man

can not be grateful to Allah either".

(Hadith: Abu Dawud)

Many people have contributed to this book. In particular, I would like to express my gratitude to Anam Zaki, who is the language editor of this book. I am also very much thankful to Dr. Farida Khanam.

With great pleasure, I express my profound sense of gratitude to my kind teacher Prof. Akhtar-ul-Wasey. I have greatly benefited by his constructive suggestions and inspiring influence.

I offer my thanks to my mother Amtul Mubin, wife Sufia Anjum and sons Hammad & Humaid who have supported me without any complaints, as usual.

Jazahum Allah fial-darayn

I dedicate this book to India.

Preface

The Necessity of Religion

All the knowledge of the world can be divided into two categories:

Acquired Knowledge: All the secular knowledge of the world (Social Sciences, Humanities and Languages, Science, Medical Science, Astronomy etc.) is acquired knowledge. This is because it is based on observation, research and analysis. It is acquired with the help of the five senses.

Revealed Knowledge: The religious scriptures are revealed. Thus, revealed knowledge is not acquired with the help of the five senses.

Acquired knowledge mainly focuses on the question - "What is Man and what is the Universe." Whereas, revealed knowledge talks about "why man is born and why does he die." Hence, the difference between both is of 'what' and 'why.'

Religion discusses the definition of man's life. In fact, it is the knowledge of self-realization. It informs us about the existence of human life. It gives answers to the ultimately crucial questions e.g., Does man have a Creator? What does

He want? Where did Man come from? Why is a man born? Where does man have to go after death? etc.

The other major difference between acquired knowledge and revealed knowledge is: The first improves the quality of our life-style (and is concerned with the human body). Whereas, the second develops the quality of man.

I am O.K.- You are O.K.

The statement - "All religions are right" is a myth. If it is to be believed, then this concept gives us two results:

1. God works uselessly: Firstly, He gave Hinduism, then Judaism, then Christianity, then Islam etc.

2. God wants to create enmity between mankind: For instance, He prohibited the Hindu from eating mutton, but permitted it for the Jew etc.

It is impossible to follow the teachings of all the religions at the same time. Hinduism is against divorce but Judaism permits it. Marriage is prohibited for a priest in Catholic Christianity, but it is appreciable for an Imam in Islam. Wealth is worshiped in Hinduism (Goddess Lakshmi) but it is condemned in Christianity.

Jainism appreciates nakedness (Digambara Sect) but Islam made it obligatory for man to cover his body. Hinduism accepts monastic life as the highest virtue, but Islam condemns it. Shaving the head, moustache and the beard is compulsory for a Buddhist monk, but in Sikhism it is absolutely prohibited. The most virtuous way for attainment of death by a Jain monk is by voluntarily abstaining from water and food. But in Islam, suicide is absolutely forbidden etc.

The conclusion is that all religions are different. Now, the question arises – why are some similarities found in all religions? e.g., all are against stealing, all advocate honesty etc.

The answer to the above question is: The source of all religions is one (God).

Here, another question arises – Then why are most of the teachings of the religions different and contradictory?

The answer to this question is: there are two categories of religions - Preserved-Religions and Non Preserved-Religions. Today, Islam is the only religion, which belongs to the first category. It has the protection-cover of God, thus no one can or will change its message (The Quran):

> "We have, without doubt sent down the Message
>
> and We will assuredly guard it".(1)

"Surely the true religion with Allah is Islam.(2) and whoever desires a religion other than Islam, it shall not be accepted from him and in the hereafter he shall be one of the losers".(3)

An Introduction to Quran

Islam

Islam is an Arabic word which is derived from the root word 'Salm' which means 'Peace', another root word of Islam is 'Silm' which means "Submission", So that, it can be said that Islam means "Acquiring peace by submitting your will to God in this world and Here-after". In religious terms, Islam means "The Submission to God". Whoever and whenever and wherever obeyed God according to the will of God, that was and is Islam. This name is given by God himself. It is the religion approved by God for human beings. It is the guidance for all mankind from God. All the Messengers / Prophets sent by God (from Adam to Muhammad) brought the same religion. Islam is the only religion for both man and the universe. The entire universe obeys God's commands. Man is supposed to do "obedience by choice" beside "obedience by compulsion".

The Prophet Muhammad

God in His infinite Mercy has selected certain individuals to communicate His message to mankind, so that all human beings might be enabled to follow the right path. These chosen people were called Prophets or Messengers. They received God's message through His angel and then conveyed it to their people.

All the prophets, according to Islam, brought the same basic truth: that there is only one God and that all human beings are accountable to God for their actions: when Doomsday finally comes, they will be judged by Him according to their good and bad deeds. Those who believe in Allah and His prophet shall be rewarded by God in the next world. While those who disbelieve shall be punished by God in the next world according to the deeds, they have performed on earth.

God's messengers came in every age and to every region, starting with Adam and ending with the Prophet Muhammad. They were human beings. The message of all the Prophets is one and the same, as Allah is one, so is His message. But the previous messages were unprotected by God, so man was able to change them but the final message (Quran) is under the protection of God, so no one can change it.

The Quran

Al- Quran is the final and preserved message of God for mankind, revealed upon the final Prophet Muhammad. The followings are the different ways, through which the message (Wahy / Revelation) came to the prophet are as follows:

- **True Dreams: whatever the Prophet dreamt in the night became true during the day.**

- **The angel (Gabriel) used to suggest directly to the heart of the Prophet, being invisible to him.**

- **Sometime the message came in the form of the ringing sound of a big bell.**

- **Coming down of the Angel in the form of a man.**

- Coming down of the Angel in his original shape.

- The message came down directly to the prophet's heart without any agency (angel or voice).

The Collection of the Quran

The Quran is a book of revelation from God. Today it exists in the form of a book consisting of 114 chapters. They were sent down by the angel Gabriel, bit by bit according to the demand of circumstances.

The revelations started in 610 A.D., while the Prophet was in seclusion in the cave of Hira mountain, two miles from Makkah. The entire revelation was completed over a period of 23 years. The last passage was revealed when the Prophet was addressing a gathering at Mount Arafat after performing farewell pilgrimage in A.D. 622.

The Quran was not revealed all at one time. It was revealed gradually over a period of twenty-three years. When any part of the Quran was revealed to the Prophet, he used to recite it to his companions. Since the verses of the Quran were recited during prayer the companions had to memorize them in order to recite them in their daily prayers.

In this way the memorization and the writing down of the Quran both started from the very first day of revelation.

According to traditions, whenever a revelation was received, Prophet called one of his scriber companions and dictated the verses to them. After dictation the Prophet also asked the scriber to read out to him what had been put in writing. This was done in order to correct any mistakes committed while writing.

This was thus the beginning of the compilation of the Quran. The next stage after writing down was to memorize the text. The Prophet himself asked the companions to memorize the revealed verses and repeat the same in their prayers.

Thus the message of the Quran was not transmitted only by oral tradition even during the lifetime of the prophet. Among his companions were a select group of about forty Katib-e-Wahy (transcribers of the revelations). Some of them are: Abu Bakr, Umar, Uthman, Ali, Zaid ibn Thabit, Maadh ibn Jabal, Ubadah ibn Samit, Abu Darda, Abu Ayyub, Ubayy ibn Ka'b etc. A few of these scribes were always present and whenever any part of the Quran was revealed, the Prophet would recite it to them. Thereupon, at the exact moment of revelation, they would not only commit it to memory, but would write it down on any available material, such as paper, bones, leather or skin. In former times when the accepted way of disseminating the subject matter of a book was to memorize it, then recite it, it was quite exceptional that the Quran should have been both memorized and preserved in writing. This was like having a 'double checking' system, whereby memory plus written words and written words plus memory could be constantly checked against each other.

The second point concerns the arrangement of the verses and chapters of the Quran. When the Quran was revealed in parts, at different times according to the demand of circumstances, how did it come to be arranged in its present form? We find the answer in books of Hadith. It has been proved form authentic traditions that the angel Gabriel, who conveyed the revelations of God to the Prophet, had himself arranged these verses. According to the traditions, each year during the month of Ramazan, the angel Gabriel came to the Prophet and recited before him all the Quranic verses revealed up till that time, in the order in which they exist today. And after listening to the recitation by the angel Gabriel, the Prophet repeated the verses in the order in which he had heard them from Gabriel. This dual process has been termed al-Irza, 'mutual presentation' in the books of Hadith.

It is also established in these books that in the last year of the Prophet's life, when the revelations had been completed, Gabriel came to the Prophet and recited the entire Quran in the existing order twice, and similarly the Prophet also recited to Gabriel the entire Quran twice. This final presentation is called al-Arz al-Akhirah in the books of hadith.

In this way, when by the help of Gabriel the Quran was fully arranged, the Prophet recited it to his companions on different occasions in the order with which we are familiar today. In this way the Quran was preserved in its present order in the memory of tens of thousands of the companions during the lifetime of the Prophet himself.

In 632 A.D. when the Prophet died at the age of 63 years, the Quran existed in two forms: one, in the memory of the several thousand companions, since they repeated the Quran daily on different occasions, having learned it by rote in what is now its present order; two, in writing- on pieces of paper and other materials used for writing in those days. These scriptures were preserved by the companions. Although not in their present order, all the parts of the Quran existed at that time in written form.

After the death of the Prophet, Abu Bakr Siddiq was appointed the first caliph. It was during his caliphate that the compilation of the Quran was carried out. Zaid ibn Thabit, the Prophet's foremost scribe, and an authority on the Quran was entrusted with this task.

The compilation was done very meticulously Zaid made an announcement that any person who has written even the smallest portion of the Quran in the presence of the Prophet Muhammad and this was witnessed by two persons must bring such written portions.

Finally the Quran was thus collected. It was compared and verified with the version of the Huffaz. His work was more a process of collection than of compilation. That is, the scattered bits and pieces of the Quran in written form were collected by him, not so that they could be assembled and bound in one volume, but so that they could be used to verify the authenticity of the Quran as memorized by countless individuals and passed on in oral tradition. Once this exact correspondence between the oral and written forms of the Quran had been established beyond any doubt, Zaid proceeded to put the verses of the Quran down on paper in their correct order. The volume he produced was then handed over to the caliph, and this remained in the custody of the Prophet's wife, Hafse. The third caliph, Osman arranged for several copies of this text to be sent to all the states and placed in central mosques where the people could prepare further copies.

In this way the message of the Quran spread further and further both through oral tradition and hand written copies until the age of the press dawned. Many printing presses were established in the Muslim world, where the beautiful calligraphy of the scriptures was reproduced after its content had been certified by memorizers of the Quran. Thus once again with the help of memorized versions and written texts, correct, authentic copies were prepared; then with the publication of these copies on a large scale, the Quran spread all over the world. It is an irrefutable fact that any copy of the Quran found in any part of the world at any time will be exactly the same as that handed down to the Muslims by the Prophet in his last days, arranged in the form still extant today.

The Quran and Man

The Holy Quran is the message of Allah. It was revealed upon the final Prophet Muhammad. It is for the guidance of all mankind. The core theme of Quran is "Man". In Quran, Allah informs about His creation plan regarding man. Its teachings present the formula of peace in worldly life, as well as in life-hereafter.

One of the names of the Quran is "Furqan", it means "Tester". It distinguishes Right from Wrong.

"The month of Ramadan in which was revealed the Quran, a guidance for mankind and clear proofs for the guidance and the criterion (between right and wrong). (4)

"O mankind! There has come to you good advice from your Lord, and a healing for that which is in your breasts, - a guidance and a mercy for the believers." (5)

The Quran is for all mankind but only a believer can benefit from it."This (Quran) is a clear insight and evidence for mankind, and a guidance and a mercy for people who have Faith with certainty."(6)

Quran is the preserved message of God; No one can make even the slightest change in it. Because God Himself has taken the responsibility to protect it.

" Verily, We, it is We Who have sent down the Dhikr (The Quran)and surely, We will guard it (from corruption)."(7

Quran is very easy to understand. Everybody can learn from it.

"And We have indeed made the Quran easy to understand and remember; then is there any who will remember (or receive admonition)?" (8)

The core theme of Quran is man. Quran explain in detail the success and failure of man in his pre death and post death life. Quran answers the ultimate questions of man, for example: from where man came? Where man has to go after death? Is there any aim of man's life? If yes, what is the way to achieve that aim? What is the definition of life? What will be after death? Is there any creator of man? If yes, what He wants? Who is perfectly successful and unsuccessful? What is right and wrong? etc.etc.

"Indeed, We have sent down for you (o mankind) a Book (The Quran) in which there is Dhikrukum (your reminder). Will you not then understand?"(9)

The Quran is the guidance of God for mankind. Its aim is to save man from darkness of evil to light of goodness.

"(This is) a Book which We have revealed unto you (o Muhammad) in order that you might lead mankind out of darkness into light by their Lord's leave to the path of the All-Mighty, the Owner of all Praise." (10)

"The total obedience of God" is the way to success in worldly

[8]

life and life Hereafter. This way is explained in Quran perfectly.

"And whosoever obeys Allah and His Messenger, fears Allah, and keeps his duty (to Him), such are the successful." (11)

Only good deeds with right faith can bring peace in both lives of man i.e. pre and after death.

"Whoever works righteousness-whether male or female-while he (or she) is a true believer (of Islamic Tawhid) Verily, to him We will give a good life(in this world), and We shall pay them certainly a reward in proportion to the best of what they used to do (i.e. Paradise in the Hereafter)." (12)

The presence of Quran is a matter of luckiness for man. Because it is the formula to success in eternal life, which starts after death.

"O mankind! There has come to you a good advice from your Lord (The Quran) and a healing for that which is in your breasts, - a guidance and a mercy for the believers. Say: In Bounty of Allah, and in His Mercy (Islam and Quran)- therein, let them rejoice. That is better than what they amass".(13)

Quran revealed upon Prophet Muhammad in very simple Arabic language. It is the message of God, which consists God's guidance for all mankind. The message of Quran is more important than its language.

The Quran is read by two aims: for being an Islamic jurist and to understand & follow guidance of God. If a person can't understand Arabic language, he can read the translation of Quran in his mother tongue. But a person who wants to be expert of Islam, it is compulsory to be an expert of Arabic language. He has to consult Quran in its original source language (Arabic). The maximum formal and informal connectivity of man with Quran is an obligatory act. That is a Furqan (Tester) and book of guidance for mankind.

Obey one, communicate yours and respect all

The Quranic religious policy in a globalised world

Obey-One

The sayings - "All religions are right" and "All religions are one" – are nothing but myths. It is absolutely impossible to follow all religions at the same time. All religions, of present time, are different in their very nature and teachings. Had they been the same in essence, it might have been possible to follow all of them in unison. Since it is not so, it becomes virtually impossible to act upon all the teachings of all the religions at a time.

For example, the Hindu religion gives extraordinary significance to wealth; there is even a Goddess of wealth (Lakshmi), who is worshipped. But Christianity condemns superfluous wealth.

Jainism (Digambara Sect) considers nakedness as the highest virtue for sages. However, Islam strictly commands covering the body parts.

The Sikh religion condemns and prohibits cutting the hair of the head, beard and moustache. Contrastingly, Buddhism

[11]

prefers shaving the hair of the head, beard and moustache; rather even makes it obligatory for Buddhist monks.

Hinduism does not permit divorce and doesn't promote widow-remarriage, but Judaism allows it.

Catholic Christianity bans marriage for the Priests, but Islam recommends it for the Imam.

Buddhism embraces monastic life as the highest virtue; however Islam condemns it and prefers a balanced social life.

In Jainism, the best path for a sage is to voluntarily avoid eating and drinking and embrace death, but Islam prohibits the same, etc. etc.

Belief in the statements, "All religions are right" and "All religions are one" has two logical implications:

Firstly, God works uselessly: At first He gave one religion; Hinduism, after that second; Buddhism, followed by the third; Christianity and afterwards the fourth; Islam, so on and so forth.

Secondly, God intends to develop enmity between mankind, He permits Muslims to be non-vegetarians, but prohibits it for the Buddhists. He prohibits 'Jhatka' food (non-halal) for the Jews but permits it for the Sikhs.

When any follower of a religion claims that he believes that all the religions are right, he is a hypocrite and a liar. If this be his belief, why is he not a Hindu, or a Christian, or a Buddhist, or a Muslim? (14)

In the field of religion, the slogan "I am O.K., you are O.K."

cannot be considered a realistic and honest approach. In fact, the sole honest, practical, realistic policy is to say **"Obey One Religion".**

According to the Quran, all the present-day religions can be placed into two groups: Preserved Religions and Non-Preserved Religions.

A religion, in which the message of God is intact in its original shape till today i.e. language and content wise, belongs to the first category.

On the contrary, a religion, which could not preserve the original message of God, due to forgetfulness or fabrication, comes under the second category.

Today, Islam is exclusively the only religion that belongs to the first category of 'Preserved Religions.' In Islam, the message of God is absolutely and accurately preserved just as it was revealed 1400 years ago. Till today, nobody can prove a minor change in it.

God gave only one religion for the success of man in the worldly life and the hereafter (15). The first man and Prophet, Adam, presented the teachings of religion (God is one, the worldly life is temporary and a test & trial for man. Life after death is eternal and Man will be rewarded or punished for his deeds committed in the world in the form of Paradise or Hell). After Adam, the people forgot or changed his message. Thus emerged the need for another prophet to convey the original message of God.

In ancient times, the means of communication and transportation were very limited and undeveloped. Mobility of the people was minimal. As a result, one Prophet came for one region and others for other areas. This process of different prophets coming to give the message of God continued till the final and last prophet Muhammad. He also presented the same teachings but in their pure form. Thus, the message of God or all the original teachings presented by different prophets over the time culminated in the shape of Islam.(16)

From Adam to Muhammad, every prophet brought the same religion i.e., the religion of God (Deen) except for one difference.

God did not protect the teachings of previous revealed books. But the final message of God, presented by Muhammad (the Quran) was, is and will be under the protection of God. He Himself took the responsibility to keep it safe and intact. As a result we see that no one has been able to change it till today. Approximately 1400 years have passed, but the Quran is available in its original and pure form. It is a clear proof of God's protection and power.

The message of God was itself more important than the prophets themselves. After the arrival of the final and the last message of God, there stands no need for any other message (because all the messages were the same and the final message "the Quran" has the protection-cover of God). The chain of prophets concluded with the coming of Prophet Muhammad. Since then and till the end, no new prophet or message will come in this world. The Quran is available in its pure form and is most sufficient for the guidance of man.

Communicate-Yours

Every Muslim bears in mind the concept of Dawah (invitation or call to the belief in Allah). Dawah is to communicate the message of the Prophet Muhammad to all the people of all times. It is, in fact, a divine task. That is why the Quran has called it 'Nusrat' of God i.e., helping the Almighty.(17)

According to the Quran, Dawah work means to make oneself 'Nasih' and 'Amin' i.e. an honest and sincere well-wisher of all.(18)

According to the belief of the Muslims, Islam is the only religion of Allah today.(19) Allah clearly announces in the Quran that He will not accept any religion except Islam.(20) He commands that a party from the believers must invite mankind to good, enjoining what is right and forbidding the wrong.(21)

The highest good, which should be shared, is faith. Any Muslim harbouring real love and true well-wishing for his fellow-beings will naturally make humble effort for the work of Dawah. To enjoin the right and forbid the evil is in essence the result of human love.(22)

God Himself assigned the believers the duty of Dawah. He says that their's is the best of nations, on the condition that they invite to God.(23) In the eyes of a Muslim, the best thing in the world is their faith (Islam).

Following Islam means ensuring success in the worldly life as well as in the life hereafter. It is impossible for a true Muslim not to invite others to Islam, if he truly believes and is a genuine well-wisher of mankind. Not inviting others to his path is counted as a sin for a Muslim. Dawah work is an obligatory duty for each and every Muslim. After identifying the right path or guidance, it is selfishness not to share it.

Actually, Dawah means invitation to Allah or call to Allah. It is, in fact, an effort to connect the people with God. All the Messengers of God came in this world to inform mankind about the creation-scheme of God regarding human beings; i.e., the aim of life, the right path for life, details of life-hereafter etc.

It is literally an unsaid moral pact among all mankind that when a person goes towards harm, others try to stop him with their all power and means. When saving the temporary body is considered a human value, why should saving the spirit from eternal hell not be considered the highest virtue? The Quran makes Dawah work obligatory on every follower of Islam through Prophet Muhammad:

"Call to your Lord; most surely you are on right way."(24)

"And who speaks better that he who calls to Allah while he himself does good, and says: I am surely of those who submit(Muslim)?"(25)

The base of Dawah is wishing well for all. Promoting good in the society is also a main objective of Dawah.(26) The Quran, however, doesn't just promote the concept, but also gives the technique for performing it. Dawah work should be done with good intention, sincerity and wisdom.

"Call to the way of your Lord with wisdom and goodly exhortation, and have disputations with them in the best manner."(27)

Dawah work must be performed in the best manner of conversation.(28) The best character or side of the individual should be exhibited.(29) The best method of dialogue ought to be adopted.(30) Taunts, comments and abuse

[16]

must be avoided at all costs. (31) It should be in the form of dialogue, not in the orthodox style of debate.(32) The gist of the discussion should gradually move from similarities to dissimilarities.(33) It must not only cover others' but near and dear also.(34)

It must be borne in mind that self- reform and inviting others to Islam is a parallel process.

Respect-All

The presentation of Islam to non-Muslims should be done after his direct or indirect consent; otherwise it might be considered the breach of privacy. After listening and pondering over the message of Islam, the listener is free to accept or reject it.

There is no compulsion in the matter of religion.(35) Disagreement should not lead to discord and we must respect other's decision. (36)

Abusing other's concept of religion is not an amiable way to reach a conclusion.(37) We continue to respect his opinion and our cooperation remains continued in every other matter e.g., social, political, economic, educational, moral etc. 'Dissent with respect' is a Quranic policy after presenting Islam. We will respect all religions even if they do not conform to what we believe.

A Muslim wants to see everyone as a Muslim. A Christian wishes to see the whole world turn into Christianity. A Buddhist desires to see every man as a Buddhist.

In fact, this desire is not a bad thing. True and selfless well wishing is behind this emotion. Inviting others towards their religion is compulsory in many religions besides Islam. They all also want to save others from eternal loss according to their own view. This is a very precious point where we, the followers of all religions, can stand together.

If the society does not accept the right of preaching and propagation of faith, the obligatory nature of this responsibility naturally creates suffocation in the minds of the followers. It will generate guilty conscious and the terrible result of this suppression will be very harmful for the individual and the society.

"Obey one religion, communicate your religion
and respect all religions"

is, as we may conclude, the only feasible and realistic formula in this contemporary, globalized world. This policy can undoubtedly bring peace in this world on the religious level.

Signs or Science

"We (Allah) will soon show them Our signs in the universe and in their own souls, until it will become quite clear to them that it is the truth".(38)

The Holy Quran is the last and preserved message of Allah. It is the book of guidance for the whole of mankind. It highly encourages "thinking", because it is the only means to derive an understanding of the truth.

Different prophets were given diverse miracles. These were according to the development and advancement of their respected ages. The Quran is the miracle of the Prophet Muhammad. Today is the age of Science, and the Quran has many verses about scientific discoveries to prove its genuineness.

However, the Quran is not a book of Science but a book of 'Signs'. The aim of such verses is to inculcate, sustain and increase the belief of mankind. Some Quranic verses that are in complete agreement with established science are as follows:

"Those who disbelieve in Our communications, We shall make them enter fire; so oft as their skins are thoroughly burned, We will change them for other skins, that they may taste the chastisement." (39)

This verse indicates the recent discovery of Science that the feeling of pain is related to the skin of man, and not the flesh.

"We have made of water everything living".(40)

According to Science, everything is made of water. The first living thing – Amoeba – is created from the water, which was one cell organism. Moreover, every living thing has almost 75% water in its components. The changes over the land occur due to water (e.g., origin of mountains, exploding volcanos, appearing islands etc.).

"And of everything We have created pairs that you may be mindful".(41) "Glory be to Him Who created pairs of all things, of what the earth grows, and of their kind and of what they do not know".(42)

It is proven fact that everything on the earth has pairs, whether it be plants, animals, or birds etc. It is amazing that even an atom has an opposite spin of Electron and Proton.

"Do not those who disbelieve see that the heavens and the earth were closed up but We have opened them". (43)

"His command, when He intends anything, is only to say to it: Be, so it is".(44)

Regarding the origin of the earth, Science says that the earth and heaven were a single unit, then a big bang took place and the evolution of all things started. According to the Big-Bang theory, that was about 20,000,000,000 years ago. The universe began with an explosive expansion of a single extremely condensed state of matter. This is precisely what the Quran states - "the heaven and earth were joined together".

"Then He directed Himself to the heaven and it is a vapor (smoke), so He said to it and to the earth: come both, willingly or unwillingly. They both said: We come willingly". (45)

The Science says: this universe was made of Helium and Hydrogen-based gases, which were moving around. In the beginning, the universe was only a combination of gases. These gases can be seen even today; these also constitute different planets.

"(Allah) made the moon therein a light, and made the sun a lamp".(46)

Every luminous object has or has not its own light. The lamp always has its own light. According to Science, the Sun has its own light, but the Moon does not have its own light, its light is the reflection of sunlight.

"And the Sun runs on to a term appointed for it; that is the measuring of the Mighty, the Wise."(47)

Science gave three theories about the Solar System: Ptolemy introduced the first in 200 A.D. It was Geo-Centric (The Earth is in the centre and all the planets of the Solar System are moving around the Earth). The second theory was given by Nicholas Copernicus, which was Helio-Centric (The Sun is in the centre and all the planets of the Solar System are revolving around the Sun). Then, the third theory was discovered by Hershel in 1800 A.D. According to him, the Sun is in the center of our Solar System and all planets revolve around the Sun. And the Sun is traveling towards an unknown destination (16-Epics) with the speed of 24000 miles per hour. This fact is already given by the Quran that the Sun is running for an appointed time.

"And He it is Who created the night and the day and the Sun and the Moon; all (orbs) travel along swiftly in their celestial spheres".(48)

Science declares: the axis of Earth is twenty three and a half degree and the Earth is revolving on its axis with the speed of 1000 miles per second. The Earth revolves at a speed of 68000 miles per hour around the Sun. The earth takes twenty-five days (approx.) to complete one rotation.

"Do they not see that We come to the land to reduce it from its out lying borders."(49)

According to Science, in the beginning a big star passed near the Sun. A part of Sun separated from it and having evolved, later on it changed into the Earth. In the beginning, the temperature of the Earth was equal to that of the Sun. With the passage of time, the Earth became cooler and this process continues. The surface of the Earth was thicker when it was hotter. As it cools down, it shrinks in size.

"Have We not made the earth as a wide expanse, and the mountains as pegs."(50)

Science proves that the earth is like an Orange. The uppermost part of earth is called "Crust". The inner part of earth is made from "Magma". And the last innermost soft part is "Core". The mountains reached within the Core and saved the earth from moving and made balance. Amazingly, the mountains work as pegs on earth.

"And you see the mountains, you think them to be solid and they shall pass away as the passing away of the cloud - the handiwork of Allah, Who has made everything thoroughly." (51)

Science confirms: the moving Magma under the earth causes earthquakes and eruption of volcanoes. This process changes the location of mountains and leads to the formation of new mountains as clouds. Mountains have hard sediments that are deeply buried in the ground, like the roots of a tree. They play a very significant role in stabilizing the earth. The discovered fossils of sea animals in the Himalayan region prove that once, the Himalaya Mountain was a sea.

"He it is Who shows you the lightning causing fear and hope."(52)

This is a scientific fact that the thunder of clouds results in the mixing of Nitrogen with the Oxygen found in air. This process makes Nitrate (NO_3), which increases the fertility of soil. We all know that NO_3 is the food for plants. So, the Quranic verse already points out that the lightning in the sky causes hope for better crops.

"And whomsoever Allah wills to guide, He opens his breast to Islam; and whomsoever He wills to send astray, He makes his breast closed and constricted, as if he is climbing up to the sky". (53)

Science verifies: As soon as we travel upward in the sky, the Oxygen (O_2) reduces. This lack of Oxygen brings suffocation in the chest. This secret has already been opened in Quran 1400 years ago.

In conclusion, we should know that the Quran was not revealed to teach Science. Such kind of science-related verses of the Quran act as a catalyst to erase any doubt a man might have about God's message.

It should also be remembered that, if ever in the future any theory changes due to advanced development in the field of science, it does not mean that the Quran is wrong; it will merely indicate our wrong implication of the verses of the Quran about that theory.

Furthermore, science cannot be taken as a yardstick to prove the authenticity of the Quran. This is because, despite the huge development in the field of science, the discoveries are very few as compared to the complex mechanism of man and unlimited ness of the Universe. One scientist rightly stated:

"We know more and more about less and less."

According to the Encyclopedia of Ignorance –

"Increase in knowledge has only increased our ignorance."

Infact, without the help of God's message, man is handicapped to find the basic answer of his mere existence i.e. why is he born?

A response to some objections on the Quran

"Men are the maintainers of women because Allah has made some of them to excel others and because they spend out of their property; the good women are therefore obedient, guarding the unseen as Allah has guarded; and (as to) those on whose part you fear desertion, admonish them and leave them alone in the sleeping-places and beat them; then if they obey you, don't seek a way against them; surely Allah is High, Great". (54)

Question: Does the Quran permit domestic violence in the form of wife beating?

Answer: The permission for beating is not an absolute commandment. It applies to a situation where a good husband is coupled with a bad wife. Symbolically, beating the wife is the second last stage a husband resorts to, before divorce. It is, in fact, an effort to save the marriage. Divorce is the last stage in a marriage when nothing else works out.

Sometimes, parents beat their children and teachers beat their students. But this cannot be adjudged to be violence or cruelty. It is only a controlled measure to save them from harm. Thus, a good husband adopts the same method in order to reform his unruly wife and to save his marriage. According to the Quran, when there are only two options:

greater evil and lesser evil, we always go for the lesser one. Hence, to save the family from a great harm of divorce, the Quran permits beating the corrupt wife. (The rules are explained in various Ahadith, e.g., never beat on the face, very light and symbolically beating etc.). It is akin to the wound resulting from an operation performed by a doctor to save his patient.

You may ask - what about the circumstance of a bad husband being coupled with a good wife?

Generally men have more muscle power than women. But if a good wife can beat her husband for his reform and to save her marriage, the Quran has no objection to it. On the contrary, she is free to divorce him (by Khula and Fasq).

You may further ask - why did the Quran not openly permit a good wife to beat her unruly husband?

If the Quran says, "Beat your husband", in other words it would mean, "Get beaten by your husband". Rules are always made for normal and general situations; the ruling changes in exceptional cases.

If a good husband is weak and the bad wife is powerful, then the above-mentioned solution would not be applied. Instead, the husband should directly go for divorce.

"There is no blame on you if you divorce women when you have not touched them or appointed for them a portion, and make provision for them, the wealthy according to his means and the straitened in circumstances according to his means, a provision according to usage; (this is) a duty on the doers of good (to others)". (55)

Question: Why is the Quran against life-long maintenance for a woman after divorce?

Answer: The Quran makes maintenance after divorce an obligatory duty on every Muslim. A Muslim husband has to afford full maintenance of his wife during the pregnancy, breast-feeding of his child, right till the attainment of adulthood of his child.

A troubled marriage goes through different stages, and the last of it is "divorce". Now, there are only three options: Divorce, Suicide, or Murder. Here, the Quran opts for divorce, which means, freedom. Any link after divorce, even if it be in the name of permanent maintenance, cuts the total freedom of a woman. She could be prone to misuse.

A man has to fulfill the compulsory responsibility of his parents, wife, sisters & brothers, children, needy relatives, and neighbors. On the contrary, a woman has no responsibility at all; even her own responsibility falls upon others. It would indeed have been injustice with a man, if he had to give life long maintenance to his wife after the divorce. In the case of remarriage, he has to give Mahr (bridal-gift), but his divorced wife would still receive Mahr.

"His command, when He intends anything, is only to say to it: Be, so it is". (56)

"And certainly We created the heavens and the earth and what is between them in six periods".(57)

Question: Why do the above verses of the Quran seemingly contradict each other?

Answer: There is not a single contradiction in the Quran. The first Quranic verse explains "the Power of Allah" i.e. nothing is impossible for Him. He can do anything anytime. He says, "Be" and it is. The second verse points out "the Method of Allah". He does everything in a planned, organized and systematic way.

"Surely We have revealed the Reminder (Quran) and We will most surely be its guardian". (58)

Question: Why should only the Quran be protected by Allah and not all the other previously revealed messages?

Answer: All previously revealed messages were for a single nation, for a specific period of time and the message was the same. There was no need to preserve them. But the Quranic message is universal and applicable till the Qiyama (the Last Day). So it has the protection-cover of Allah.

The previous revealed books are not in a pure form today; they have been corrupted or some have even disappeared. They were for a particular time and space and all were local messages as Allah says about Hz. Isa:

"(Allah) will make him (Isa) a messenger to the Israelites". (59)

Even the New Testament highlights:

"(Jesus said) I was sent only to the lost sheep of the house of Israel".(60)

"These twelve (disciples) Jesus sent out with the following

instructions: Go nowhere among the Gentiles (Non-Jews) and enter no town of Samaritans, but go rather to the lost sheep of the house of Israel". (The book of Matthew, 10:5-6)

"None shall touch it (Quran) save the purified ones".(61)

"The month of Ramadan in which was revealed the Quran, a guidance for mankind and clear proofs for the guidance and the criterion (between right and wrong). (62)

"(This is) a Book which We have revealed unto you (o Muhammad) in order that you might lead mankind out of darkness into light by their Lord's leave to the path of the All-Mighty, the Owner of all Praise." (63)

Question: On the one hand, the Quran says: it is for the whole universe, but at the same time it commands: don't touch except purified ones. How can both things be fulfilled together?

Answer: There is a big misunderstanding in the interpretation of this verse (64) of the Quran. This verse is not about the worldly Quran; rather it refers to the lauh-e-mehfuz Quran, which is guarded by angels. If we take this verse to be about the worldly Quran, then it will be proved wronged since every bad person can purchase and touch it.

The Prophet (PBUH) sent a letter to the King of Iran (Khusro Parvez). The letter contained the verse (3:64) of the Quran, which was dictated by the Prophet. The King read the letter and tore it. Even after this event, the Prophet kept sending letters to other non-Muslims. Thus, it is a myth that the Quranic verses can be disrespected.

"Let not the believers take the disbelievers for their friends in preference to the believers. He who does this has no help from Allah, unless you guard yourselves against them, taking a precaution". (65)

Question: Why does the Quran forbid the friendship of believers with disbelievers?

Answer: Here, the correct translation of the Arabic word "Wali" is protector, not friend. The Quran prefers the protection of a believer to that of a disbeliever in the hour of need when there is a choice between two options: protection by a believer and protection by a disbeliever. The friendship of believers with disbelievers is not prohibited in the Quran. Rather it says:

"Allah does not forbid you to be kind and equitable to those who have neither made war on your religion nor driven you from your homes. Allah loves the equitable. Allah only forbids you to make friends with those who have fought against you on account of your religion and driven you from your homes or abetted others to do so. Those who make friends with them are wrongdoers". (66)

"And certainly We have created for hell many of the jinn and the men; they have hearts with which they do not understand, and they have eyes with which they do not see, and they have ears with which they do not hear; they are as cattle, nay they are in worse errors; these are the heedless ones".(67)

Question: According to the Quran the act of thinking is done by the heart. But established science states the opposite to it.

Answer: In the Quran, the term "Heart" is used in its literal meaning, not in the biological sense. The Quranic term "heart" is the equivalent to the word "Mind" of medical science. Both are applied for the same use. In all the religions and literature of the world, the term heart is used to refer to the mind. The Quran says:

"When Our communications are recited to him (disbeliever), he says: stories of those of yore. Nay! rather, what they used to do has become like rust upon their hearts".(68)

"And they say: our hearts are covered. Nay, Allah has cursed them on account of their unbelief; so little it is that they believe". (69)

"Surely those who disbelieve, it being alike to them whether you warn them, or do not warn them, will not believe. Allah has set a seal upon their hearts and upon their hearing and there is a covering over their eyes, and there is a great punishment for them". (70)

Question: *Is it not injustice of Allah that He limits the understanding of some people and then punishes them?*

Answer: Allah's style of presenting a fact is different from the style of man. Allah never does injustice. Allah created the man and universe and He made laws for each and every thing of the world. They are called law of nature.

For instance, when two atoms of Hydrogen combine with one atom of Oxygen, they make Water. A man explains this fact in these words, "The formation of water occurs due to the nature's law of H_2O".

But when Allah explained this reality, He said: "We made water". (Because the creator of Hydrogen, Oxygen and of the principle that H_2O will make water, is Allah. So, all credit goes to Him.)

Allah made the law of nature and called them His work. Whatever happens by law of nature, it comes into existence by the Will of Allah.

According to the law of nature, the heart (mind) of disbelievers was opened to receive the guidance of Allah in the beginning. But they did not follow the law of guidance; they refused again and again and persisted in sins. As a result, they invited the seal of darkness. So, their hearts became rigid and sealed from receiving the guidance. It is to be seen clearly that nowhere is a man's freedom of choice curtailed.

"They (your wives) are a garment for you and you are a garment for them". (71)

"Your wives are a tilth for you". (72)

Question: Do the above-mentioned verses of the Quran contradict each other?

Answer: Tea is made from tealeaf. Tea is prepared by milk. Both these statements do not disagree with each other. The same is with the above-stated verses. The relationship of a husband and wife is beautifully explained here in a symbolic way.

Men and women are each other's garments: i.e., they provide each other mutual support, mutual comfort, and mutual protection, comforting each other as a garment comforts the body. A garment is also for both - show and concealment.

Moreover, a wife is compared to a husband's tilth; his relationship with her is a serious affair to him. He sows the seed in order to reap the harvest. But he chooses his own time and mode of cultivation. He does not sow out of season nor does he cultivate in a manner which will injure or exhaust the soil. He is wise and considerate and does not run riot.

"Praise be to Allah, who created the heavens and the earth, who made the angels, messengers with wings — two or three, or four. He adds to His creation as He pleases: for Allah has power over all things". (73)

"Surely the strategy of the Satan is weak". (74)

Question: Man can never understand the accurate nature of angels and Satan. Then, why does a Muslim have to believe in them?

Answer: Man always associates two things with God: Visible things (sun, sea, moon, mountain etc.) and invisible things (air etc.).

A man saves himself from polytheism when he believes in Angels and Satan. When a man gets a benefit or harm which is by an invisible force, he can say: it is Angel's or Satan's work. This belief makes the concept of Tawhid (oneness and uniqueness of Allah) pure and perfect.

"Praise be to Allah, the Cherisher and Sustainer of the worlds; Most Gracious, Most Merciful". (75)

"Whoever comes to his Lord (being) guilty, for him is surely hell; he shall not die therein, nor shall he live". (76)

Question: Allah is merciful, why will He put people in hell?

Answer: This situation should be seen in the framework of Justice, not mercy. If a criminal is left scot-free then it would entail injustice with the innocent. In fact, justice is the result or consequence of mercy.

"You (Muslims) are the best of the nations". (77)

Question: Are the Muslims privileged and special community in the sight of Allah?

Answer: The word 'Muslim' is an action-based term rather than being name-based or just a label. A person becomes a Muslim due to his good deeds (right beliefs are included here). Everybody can be a Muslim on the basis of his right conduct. The above verse is not quoted completely. The complete verse is –

"You are the best of the nations raised up for (the benefit of) man; you enjoin what is right and forbid the wrong and believe in Allah". (78)

Muslims have a conditional status in the eyes of Allah. They are responsible for communicating Allah's message to the world. They are privileged from this angle, but it is not a privilege of specialty but that of responsibility and accountability.

"We (Allah) did not send before you (Muhammad) any but men to whom We sent revelation". (79)

Question: Why did Allah not send a woman as a prophet?

Answer: Every position depends on two things: Status and Responsibility. Perhaps, having no female prophet could be looked down upon as an injustice when we see it from the status point of view. But it can be justified when we view it from the responsibility point of view.

Allah gave the responsibility of childbirth and upbringing to women, a non-optional duty. This big responsibility exempted her from all kinds of other responsibilities i.e., trade, war etc. As we know, big responsibility brings big concession.

Moreover, communicating the Message of Allah to people was not an easy task. For a woman, it would have been difficult during menses and pregnancy. Generally women are relatively physically weak, so they might be subjected to harassment and rape.

"So when the sacred months have passed away, then slay the idolaters wherever you find them, and take them captives and besiege them and lie in wait for them in every ambush". **(80)**

Question: Does the Quran permit Muslims to kill non-Muslims?

Answer: A Military General has only three options of command in a battlefield. First, kill the enemy. Second, be killed by the enemy. Third, run away from the battlefield. Obviously, every able and sensible general would choose the first option.

The same thing is mentioned in the Quranic chapter-9 & verse-5, which was related to the battlefield. Allah commanded His believers to kill their enemies in the battlefield.

The above-mentioned verse is mentioned out of context. The complete context can be understood based on verses 1 to 7.

Actually, there was a treaty between believers and disbelievers. The disbelievers broke the treaty unilaterally. Allah gave them four months time to reform. They did not change themselves, so the war was declared on them. The state of peace thus, was converted into state of war.

Moreover, every enemy was free to hear the Word of Allah, in spite of their distrustfulness. The duty was assigned to the believers to protect them and ensure their return to their place of safety.

"(This is a declaration of) immunity by Allah and His Apostle towards those of the idolaters with whom you made an agreement. So go about in the land for four months and know that you cannot weaken Allah and that Allah will bring disgrace to the unbelievers. And an announcement from Allah and His Apostle to the people on the day of the greater pilgrimage that Allah and His Apostle are free from liability to the idolaters; therefore if you repent, it will be better for you, and if you turn back, then know that you will not weaken Allah; and announce painful punishment to those who disbelieve. Except those of the idolaters with whom you made an agreement, then they have no failed you in anything and have not backed up any one against you, so fulfill their agreement to the end of their term; surely, Allah loves those who are careful (of their duty). So when the sacred months have passed away, then slay the idolaters wherever you find them, and take them captives and besiege them and lie in wait for them in every ambush, then if they repent and keep up prayer and pay the poor-rate, leave their way free to them; surely Allah is Forgiving, Merciful. And if one of the idolaters seek protection from you, grant him protection till he hears the word of Allah, then make him attain his place of safety; this is because they are a people who do not know. How can there be an agreement for the idolaters with Allah and with His Apostle; except those with whom you made an agreement at the Sacred Mosque? So as long as they are true to you, be true to them; surely Allah loves those who are careful) of their duty). (81)

"And if you fear that you cannot act equitably towards orphans, then marry such women as seem good to you, two and three and four; but if you fear that you will not do injustice (between them), then (marry) only one or what your right hand possess; this is more proper, that you may not deviate from the right course". (82)

Question: Does Quran recommend polygamy over monogamy?

Answer: Marriage is not made obligatory in the Quran. But it is highly preferable. If there is physical ability plus economic eligibility and no control of the baser self in a man; then marriage is compulsory (with choice) for him. But, if there is physical ability plus economic eligibility and control; marriage is highly appreciated. However, if there is physical eligibility with no economic eligibility; marriage is unadvisable (fasting is prescribed). And if there is no physical eligibility; marriage is prohibited.

When there are only two options: Marriage and No-Marriage; Islam chooses marriage. Also, when there are other two options: Monogamy and Polygamy; Islam opts for Monogamy. But, if the options are: Polygamy and Sexual Anarchy; Islam very sensibly selects Polygamy. We have to note that it is permitted only with the condition of justice.

The Quran is the only one religious book among all available revealed scriptures, which prescribes Monogamy.

"Call to the way of your Lord with wisdom and goodly exhortation, and have disputations with them in the best manner".(83)

Question: Has the Quran permitted the quarreling between Muslims and Non-Muslims during a religious discussion?

Answer: The Quran is in favor of the policy that religion is a matter of free choice for man. The Quran says: there is no compulsion in religion. (84) All kinds of compulsions and pressures are prohibited in order to attract a person to religion. The Quran teaches its believers to argue, not quarrel in a religious discussion and that too in a healthy manner and convince the opponent with wise arguments. In fact, both – quarrel and argument - are quite distinct from each other:

Quran is in favor of arguing, not quarrelling. Both are very different to each other. The reasoning or arguing is rational, factual, fair, consistent, while the reasoning of quarrelling is emotional, embellished, biased & contradictory. Furthermore, the mood of arguing is calm, reasonable, objective & mature, whereas the mood of quarreling is turbulent, angry, subjective & childish. Moreover, the aim of arguing is to discover truth, knowledge, opponent's respect, however the aim of quarreling is to win points, status and opponent's defeat.

"She came to her people with him (Isa), carrying him (with her). They said: O Maryam! Surely you have done a strange thing. O sister of Haroun! Your father was not a bad man, nor was your mother an unchaste woman".(85)

[38]

Question: *There is more than a thousand year gap between Haroun and Maryam. But according to the Quran, Maryam was the sister of Haroun, is it not against historical fact?*

Answer: The term "Ukhta" can be used in both meanings; sister as well as descendent, depending upon the context. The translation of "Ukhta Haroun" is not correct in the above-mentioned verse. A person who knows the Arabic language can easily understand that here "Ukhta Haroun" means "descendent of Haroun" and not the sister of Haroun. And it is a historical fact.

This is the normal style of the language, as we see in Bible also:

"He (Christ) was the son of Joseph".(86)

"Jesus, the Messiah, the son of David". (87)

According to the above-mentioned Bible verses, Jesus had two fathers: Joseph and David. But that cannot be correct. However, we may understand it correctly, when we study it in context. Here 'son' denotes "descendent", i.e. descendent of Joseph and David. Another example from Bible may be - "His (Zechariah) wife was a descendent of Aaron, and her name was Elizabeth". (88)

Some Quranic concepts

The understanding of any religion is not possible without the awareness of its basic concepts. In order to comprehend Islam in a better way, we must go through the root differences between contemporary practices and the Islamic concept. The following article is an effort to briefly define the Quran-based foundations of Islam:

Deen v/s Duniya

Worldly life (duniya) is not against religious life (deen). The proper and effective utilization of worldly life is infact, a religious life. There is absolutely no contradiction between them.

Materialism v/s Material Prosperity

Islam is not against material prosperity. Rather, it holds that material wealth heralds the opportunity to acquire more and more virtues. It is helpful to achieve the aim of life i.e., God's pleasure. But it maintains a firm stand against engrossing materialism, since materialism changes the very goal of life and man spends an animal-like life, thus it is not liked in Islam.

Spiritualism v/s Materialism

Spirituality means "Rabbaniat" i.e., to be a devoted servant of God. Islam highly preferred God-oriented life.We may say that spirituality is 'the impact of Godliness on human life'. But, Materialism gives preference to material life rather than worship and devotion to God, thus it is condemned. However, Islam firmly establishes that the proper use of materialistic life makes man spiritualistic.

Taqdir v/s Effort

There are two things related to Taqdir (destiny):

1. *Nature and Knowledge of destiny*

2. *Belief in destiny*

To me, Taqdir (destiny) refers to the knowledge of God. We have to acknowledge that understanding, the very nature and grasping the absolute knowledge of Taqdir is impossible for man. It would be akin to pouring two liters of milk in a one-liter bottle. Meaning, it is not possible for man to fully understand this concept with his limited capabilities. But belief in Taqdir is useful for man. The concept of Taqdir credits success and failure to God, which saves man from pride in the case of success and depression in the face of failure, saving him from being suicidal.

Knowledge v/s Practice

There is no difference between knowledge and practice. Knowledge is a form of practice. Infact, we may say that knowledge is a superior form of practice. A person, who is doing a good act without it being in his knowledge, is not better than a person who does not do a good act even when he has knowledge of it. The first person is prone to sin. Neither can he instruct others about it nor make any reform. But it is supposed that someday the first one will stop from sin.

Gaining knowledge is also an activity. In the pursuit of knowledge and research, we abstain from luxuries and work hard. Actually the combination of both the things is recommended in Islam. Forty five verses of Quran declare that to combine faith (right knowledge) with good deeds guarantees success in worldly life as well as in the hereafter.

Best v/s Average

Most of the time, most people are trapped in a wicked net – they decide that either we will perform the highest religious act in the best way or not perform any religious act at all. For example, perfect prayer or no prayer at all. But, Islam very beautifully says that whenever one has a choice between two evils: one greater evil and the other lesser evil, a person should choose the lesser one. Yes, it does mean that if there are two options, one perfect prayer and the other imperfect prayer, we should prefer the perfect one. But if the options are imperfect prayer and no prayer at all, we must adopt the former than the latter.

Anti-body attitude v/s Pro-body attitude

The human body is an 'Amanat' of God. Consequently, since it belongs to someone else, we have no right to kill or torture ourselves. Self-rights are very important. If a person is not fulfilling the rights of his body, he would not be considered a good person in the Eyes of God; he will be accountable for it and will be questioned regarding it on the Day of Judgment.

Socialization v/s Monastic-life

This life is an examination, a test. A person's social life, his interactions and dealings with others become the criteria to judge him. Moreover, isolation from society proves to be a big barrier in human development. Having no social life is like escaping from the exam and is a revolt against God's Scheme of creation of man.

Balance v/s Extremism

Imam Nawawi says: We never see any imbalance which does not disturb the rights of others e.g., when a person tends to his wife completely, the rights of his mother are curbed, vis-à-vis. An extremist is harmful for himself as well as for the society. According to Islam, every one is responsible for his each and every action in this world. The key to success lies in balance.

His character was the Quran

The Prophetic Morality

The Quran is the book of guidance for whole mankind. It explains the creation scheme of the Creator regarding man. Man can understand the aim of his life through the Quran. The Last Prophet Muhammad was the embodiment of Quranic teachings. The message of the Quran is the morality of the Prophet, which is relevant for every period and time, even in the 21st century, too.

Moral means "principles of right and wrong" and morality implies "a particular system of moral principles" while the Prophetic morality denotes "a particular system of Prophetic moral principles, which is absolutely based on the Quran."

The Prophetic Morality is Divine and religion-based. It is not the result of experience, observation and research. It is purely God-gifted and God-oriented, which prepares man for leading a God-centered life. It completely harmonizes with human nature. The Creator of man and the Giver of morality is God. So no contradiction is found here.

The morality for the sake of morality is not the type of Prophetic morality. It is in fact the morality based on religion (Islam). It doesn't mind to keep expectations only from God and not from man. As a result, the frustration in case of not returning the reward of good deeds cannot make man its victim. Because the return is confirmed from God Almighty. The follower of Prophetic morality never loses his heart.

The Prophetic Morality adopts a holistic approach to life. It declares that everything is related with each other. The moral aspect of life affects the social aspect; social aspect influences economic aspect; economic aspect changes psychological aspects of life, so forth and so on. Man is treated a single unit and every part of man's life is inter-related and inter-mingled.

It is universal morality. It gives the concept of blood-based equality between mankind. Adam was the father of all mankind, so no difference is found on the basis of color, caste or creed. The only one thing, which can bring distinction between different people, is taqwa (piety). A pious person is more superior to a non-pious, in the eyes of God. No other criterion is accepted, appreciated or considered valuable by God.

The claim of tongue is worthless without the deed. Contradiction between saying and deed is hypocrisy. The Prophetic teachings point out that Iman is the combination of these three things: acceptance of the tongue, conviction of the heart and action by the body.

The Prophetic Morality is single-track-morality. What others do is not the behaviour-moulder of a man. Everyone is writing his own examination paper. No one will be asked about other's deeds. A person should do good if others do good to him; but he should not do injustice if others don't do justice to him. To repel evil with good is the formula of this system.

When a person follows the above-mentioned system, the

self-corrective-mechanism starts automatically. Because it wants to bring reform in man from inner-self to outer-self. The beliefs are the driving force behind actions. The beliefs of oneness and uniqueness of God (Tawhid) and life-hereafter (Akhirah) change the world-view of man. The mental canvas of man enlarges, as a result the broad-heartedness and broad-mindedness appears in behavior of the followers.

Another feature of this system is "Downward-Comparison" in worldly affairs, but with utmost efforts. When a person accepts the result of his efforts, he not only saves him from depression, frustration and pessimism but also maintains the balance in the society.

This Prophetic Morality not only discusses the rights and duties of a person, but also highlights the fundamental prohibitions. The clear concept of permissible and prohibited is given in it. This prohibited list is not very large. It is very easy to escape from it.

Obedience can be conditional and unconditional. The unconditional obedience is only and exclusive right of God. All other types of obedience must be conditional. There is no obedience in evil; only good act will be obeyed.

There is no difference between worldly and religious life. The proper utilization of worldly life is Deen (religion). The Prophetic Morality favors material prosperity in comparison with materialism. As well as spiritual life is also the part of social life. Full socialization develops spirituality in man, but the condition is it must be God-oriented. It must be absolutely anti-monastic in its approach and attitude.

The Prophetic Morality fulfils all necessities and trains man to control his desires. The control over the body parts is stressed in this system. The body is considered a precious gift of God and the life is an examination, with the help of the body and its faculties; man has to clear this worldly test and trial. The anti-body attitude of man corrupts all the aim; so suicide is absolutely prohibited.

According to this morality, the combination of moral power and material power brings justice in the society. This time the balance of the world has been disturbed. On who has moral power does not own sufficient material power, and whoever has material power does not have moral power. So, some are weak and honest and the others are strong and corrupt.

This morality adopts universal approach. Each good thing (wisdom) is everyone's property. Human experience is separated from religious commandments. To clear all barriers in the way of development, only the Prophet is the recommended model of God, all others are teachers. Man can learn good things from everyone.

In conclusion, the Prophetic Morality is the solution of all contemporary problems. Because all other religious moralities give the slogan, e.g., justice and peace should be in the society and world, but how? No one gives the complete formula, except the Prophetic Morality, i.e. Islam.

Seven great hurdles in the way of truth

"Conjecture can never be a substitute for Truth".(89)

Those who sincerely seek the Truth keep their minds open and seek it earnestly. But, there are certain hurdles that obstruct this enquiry and may restrict the individual and bar them from reaching the Truth.

1. Arrogance

Arrogance here doesn't mean, as generally perceived, pride over material possessions, beauty etc. Rather, as the hadith in Muslim states: "Arrogance means ridiculing and rejecting the Truth and despising people." Consequently, it is a big obstacle in the way of Truth. Allah, the Almighty states:

"Those who behave arrogantly on the earth in defiance of right - them will I turn away from My signs: Even if they see all the signs, they will not believe in them; and if they see the way of right conduct, they will not adopt it as the way; but if they see the way of error, that is the way they will adopt. For they have rejected our signs, and failed to take warning from them". (90)

2. Wealth

Acquiring wealth is not condemned in Islam. Material prosperity is encouraged against materialism in Islam. The excessive love and obsession of wealth can easily blind a person, make him proud and lead him astray as he may then conceive himself to be superior and self-reliant.

" Never did We send a warner to a population, but the wealthy ones among them said: "We believe not in the (Message) with which ye have been sent. They said: We have more in wealth and in sons, and we cannot be punished. Say: Verily my Lord enlarges and restricts the Provision to whom He pleases, but most men understand not. It is not your wealth nor your sons, that will bring you nearer to Us in degree: but only those who believe and work righteousness - these are the ones for whom there is a multiplied Reward for their deeds, while secure they (reside) in the dwellings on high!" (91)

3. Considering worldly fortune as a criterion of virtue

Generally, people consider good luck to be a sign of blessing, virtue and prosperity and to link bad luck or misfortune with punishment of the Lord or disgrace in the world. When we are at the receiving end of something good, we credit ourselves for it and tend to blame God for our hardships. This makes us shortsighted and haughty.

"But people have cut off their affair (of unity), between them, into sects: each party rejoices in that which is with itself. But leave them in their confused ignorance for a time. Do they think that because We have granted them abundance of wealth and sons, We would hasten them on in every good? Nay, they do not understand".(92)

"Now, as for man, when his Lord trieth him, giving him honour and gifts, then saith he, (puffed up), My Lord hath honoured me. But when He trieth him, restricting his subsistence for him, then saith he (in despair), "My Lord hath humiliated me!".(93)

4. Reliance on speculation more than true knowledge

Mere speculation can never be equivalent to the truth. Yet, most merely follow conjecture and what-could-be or might-be. This creates room for doubt and no logical conclusion can be reached. Any thoughts built up on 'suppositions' are bound to be faulty and defective.

"Wert thou to follow the common run of those on earth, they will lead thee away from the way of Allah. They follow nothing but conjecture: they do nothing but lie." (94)

"Say: Of your 'partners' is there any that can give any guidance towards truth? Say: It is Allah Who gives guidance towards truth, is then He Who gives guidance to truth more worthy to be followed, or he who finds not guidance (himself) unless he is guided? What then is the matter with you? How judge ye? But most of them follow nothing but fancy: truly fancy can be of no avail against truth. Verily Allah is well aware of all that they do".(95)

5. Blind following of ancestors

Perhaps one of the most deadly and persistent roadblocks in the way of finding out the Truth is blind following of ancestors. It cripples the mind, soul and comprehension of an individual and is a fierce barrier in the way of free will and independent thought.

"Their apostles said: Is there a doubt about Allah, The

Creator of the heavens and the earth? It is He Who invites you, in order that He may forgive you your sins and give you respite for a term appointed!" They said: "Ah! Ye are no more than human, like ourselves! Ye wish to turn us away from the (gods) our fathers used to worship: then bring us some clear authority." (96)

"Just in the same way, whenever We sent a Warner before thee to any people, the wealthy ones among them said: "We found our fathers following a certain religion, and we will certainly follow in their footsteps." (97)

"When they do aught that is shameful, they say: We found our fathers doing so; and (Allah) commanded us thus: Say: Nay, Allah never commands what is shameful: do ye say of Allah what ye know not?" (98)

6. Wrong Beliefs

Often, people harbour wrong beliefs. Be it due to tradition, misinformation, ignorance or pure mischief. They do not make the effort to ratify their beliefs according to rational thought and neither do they verify them as per the established facts.

"Is it not to Allah that sincere devotion is due? But those who take for protectors other than Allah (say): "We only serve them in order that they may bring us nearer to Allah." Truly Allah will judge between them in that wherein they differ. But Allah guides not such as are false and ungrateful."(99)

"They serve, besides Allah, things that hurt them not nor profit them, and they say: "These are our intercessors with Allah." Say: "Do ye indeed inform Allah of something He knows not, in the heavens or on earth? - Glory to Him! And far is He above the partners they ascribe (to Him)!"(100)

7. Misguided Leadership

The world comprises of more followers than leaders. Understandably, it is only a few who can lead the masses; otherwise it would lead to complete chaos. But, when this very leadership is misguided and erroneous, it consequently, ends up misguiding the masses who often obey it blindly.

"The Day that their faces will be turned upside down in the Fire, they will say: Woe to us! Would that we had obeyed Allah and obeyed the Messenger. And they would say: "Our Lord! We obeyed our chiefs and our great ones, and they misled us as to the (right) Path. Our Lord! Give them double Penalty and curse them with a very great Curse!" (101)

Rabbaniat: Quranic Spirituality

"Be people of the Lord" *(102)*

Spirituality is referred to as "Rabbaniat" in the Quran (Be people of the Lord). Rabbaniat involves focusing one's mind on God. 'Rabbani' is a person whose thinking and actions are God-oriented, one who has placed God as the center of his attention and he is able, in the words of the Prophet, "to see with God's eye, to speak with God's tongue, to walk with God's foot and to hear with the ear of God".

In other words, we may say that Rabbaniat or spirituality is the impact of Godliness on man's life, which transforms the inner self and is expressed through the outer self. Now, the question is - how can a person develop Rabbaniat in himself?

The answer is simple: By reflection and meditation/ 'tafakkur wa tadabbur'(103) It is an intellectual process which, according to the Quran, has two different directions: 'al-anfus' and 'al-afaq.' Anfus literally means the body & spirit of man i.e. the inner world; afaq literally means the universe, i.e. the external world.

When a person observes that the universe functions in a perfect manner and finds that all the events in this vast universe always proceed towards a significant result; he concludes that man must also have a Creator and his life should also have a meaningful end.

A question arises here: Why do some people lead a materialistic life but others spend a monastic life in the name of spirituality?

In order to understand this, let us consider the following example: There are twins. One is alive and the other is dead. Both are identical in their physical appearance. However, the twin who is alive has something that the dead one does not; he lacks something that stops his movements. This missing thing is the 'spirit'. The spirit is a subjective entity, which cannot be explained in objective terms.

Man is a combination of body and spirit. We may say (symbolically) that the human body is brought to life on this planet, thus it is inclined towards the earth and it has beastly tendencies e.g., revenge, anger, hate, violence and selfishness etc. On the other hand, the human spirit comes from heaven and so has a heavenly-inclination. It follows that it has angelic features e.g., forgiveness, tolerance, sacrifice, love, selflessness and peace etc.

Spirit and body are quite contradictory to each other. They lean towards two opposite directions. As a result, man experiences a constant struggle within himself right till his death. Eventually, this struggle leads to three possible outcomes:

1. **The body overpowers the spirit**
   (consequently, man spends a materialistic life.)

2. **The spirit overpowers the body**
   (consequently, man spends a monastic life.)

3. **Establishment of balance between the body and spirit.**

The last one is, evidently, the perfect and ideal stage. All Islamic teachings train man to attain this situation. Belief in God and following His commands maintain a balance between the body and the spirit. On the contrary, the first and the second outcomes are condemned in the Quran in the following vein:

"Seest thou such a one as taketh for his god his own passion (or impulse)? Couldst thou be a disposer of affairs for him? Or thinkest thou that most of them think and understand? They are only like cattle; - nay, they are worse astray in path."(104)

"Say: Who hath forbidden the beautiful (gifts) of Allah, which He hath produced for His servants, and the things, clean and pure, (which He hath provided) for sustenance? Say: They are, in the life of this world, for those who believe, (and) purely for them on the Day of Judgment." (105)

Misfortune

"Whatever affliction befalls you, it is on account of what your hands have wrought." (106)

"No evil befalls on the earth nor in your own souls, but it is in a book before We bring it into existence; surely that is easy to Allah: So that you may not grieve for what has escaped you, nor be exultant at what He has given you; And Allah does not love any arrogant boaster."(107)

The notion of a 'safe life' is an illusion for man on this planet. No man has, or had, or will have an absolutely secure life. The quest for a life without misfortune is pointless. All misfortunes that befall man may be placed in the following two categories:

1. *Invite-Misfortune*

2. *Determined-Misfortune*

A young man drove rashly and as a result, his car met with an accident.

An old man over-ate and consequently became the victim of food poisoning. Such misfortunes are invited by man himself. Thus, they may be termed as "Invited Misfortune."

Now, the father of that wounded young man borrowed money for the treatment of his son. The wife of that ill old man took great pains in taking care of her husband. Such kinds of misfortunes befell the father and the wife without any fault of their own. And they may be named - "Determined Misfortune."

The first kind of misfortune is the result of man's own bad deeds. But the second is meant as a trial for him, as a test of man. God wants to see that when a person is trapped in 'determined misfortune', will he keep patience or would he complain? The patient one would be rewarded and the latter would be punished.

The formula for safety from 'invited misfortune' lies in the statement - "precaution is better than cure".

But, on the contrary, no matter how clever you are, you can never save yourself from 'determined misfortune.' Only increased "resistance" enables you to face it and can reduce the pain. However, there is a formula that helps in such a situation. We may understand it from the statement that "A big problem makes a small problem seem a trifle or little". Thus, as much as the life of the hereafter is remembered, the problems of the worldly life are belittled and reduced. Moreover, a man should always remember:

"We (Allah) do not impose on any soul a duty except to the extent of its ability". (108)

According to the Quran, all misfortunes that befall man have the following three factors behind them:

ˣ **As a punishment of sins:**

"Whatever affliction befalls you, it is on account of what your hands have wrought." (109)

* **As a warning:**

"We seized them with distress and affliction in order that they might humble themselves." (110)

* **For the test & trial of man:**

"And We (Allah) will most certainly try you with somewhat of fear and hunger and loss of property and lives and fruits." (111)

The above-mentioned factors may also be understood to be behind all fortunes of man i.e., for reward, as a warning and for trial.

Intelligence

"Verily! In the creation of the heavens and the earth, and in the alternation of night and day, and the ships which sail through the sea with that which is of use to mankind, and the water (rain) which Allah sends down from the sky and makes the earth alive therewith after its death, and the moving (living) creatures of all kinds that He has scattered therein, and in the veering of winds and clouds which are held between the sky and the earth, are indeed Ayah (proofs, evidences, signs, etc.) for people of the understanding". (112)

Among every faculty that man has been bestowed with, one of the best is "Intelligence". But, this intelligence is not perfect or absolute. It can't work beyond a particular frame of time and space. For instance,

A person says, "A battle was fought between Japan and America. However, it came to blows neither before nor after the 18th century and it wasn't fought in any other century either".

A person says, "There is a country that is neither on earth nor on water, nor in the sky but it does exist".

Such things cannot be understood by our intellect. Human intelligence can never perceive a circle without a center and a triangle without an angle. It cannot visualize a fourth direction except length, width and depth.

In fact, intelligence is so restricted that it cannot recognize anything unusual. For instance, Hammad sang a song that smelt like rose, or the color of this perfume is blue etc.

Moreover, human intelligence is not able to comprehend all things of the past, present and the future. It is so limited that it cannot even understand the reality of man - i.e., Spirit.

A person ponders over his existence and reflects on the ultimate questions of his life. He arrives at the conclusion that there are two options: first, to believe in a Creator or second, not to believe in a Creator.

Now, human intelligence recognizes that almost everything in the world (pen, copy, table, chair, car, aeroplane etc.) has a creator, so why won't man, who is more advanced and sophisticated, have a Creator?

Moreover, our intelligence asserts that millions and billions years have passed and yet, the children of men are born as men, not as cats or dogs or monkeys. This also proves that the birth of man is not accidental but is well planned. Thus, the first finding of intelligence is that "Man has a Creator".

Now, our intelligence reflects more, and arrives at two subsequent options - One, Creator is single or two; there exist more than one Creator.

Here, intelligence compares following situations with two options each: A country with a Prime Minister or a country with two Prime Ministers, a class with a teacher or a class with three teachers and a car with a driver or a car with four drivers.

It reaches the conclusion that the first option in each of the situations makes the system smooth, whereas the second brings chaos. Thus, the second finding of intelligence is that "Man has only one Creator".

The intelligence further contemplates and again finds two options: First; Man should establish contact with his Creator and learn the aim of his life. Or second; the Creator should contact man and furnish him with the knowledge as to why He created man?

At this juncture, human intelligence draws the conclusion that the first option is impossible for man as he has no source or means to contact his Creator. But, the second option is possible and it is rather just and fair that it should be so.

The Creator is obviously more powerful than His creation, so He should establish contact with man and inform him about the aim of his existence. Consequently, intelligence draws the conclusion that "It is the Creator who must contact man".

On further contemplation, human intelligence again stands at two crossroads: one, the Creator should contact all people individually and inform everyone about Him and His Plan of Creation for man. Second, the Creator should make contact with some chosen people, and disclose to them His plan for man and then assign the duty to these select people to deliver His message to all human beings.

At this point, our intellect senses that if the Creator has made the worldly life of man as a test and trial for him, then He should not adopt the first means of communication. This is because it would provide surety of the existence of the Creator. Thus, the question paper would leak out before the exam, rendering it useless. It would also curtail the freedom of choice and free will granted to man to believe in God or not. On the other hand, if the Creator would adopt the second option, the world would be an example of a fair examination.

Additionally, God would also have fulfilled His responsibility to inform some people about His message and make them a means to convey to the people their aim of existence. Hence, the choice to believe in God or not would remain in the hands of man and the option of 'obeying God without seeing' would also be in his control.

Thus, the intelligence reaches the fourth conclusion that; "The Creator contacted some people (Prophets) and revealed His message to them that consisted of His scheme for man. He gave them the responsibility to convey His message to all the people. So, the worldly life became an examination for man, and he received the message and also got the freedom to obey or reject."

Further, the intelligence also arrives at the fifth conclusion that "the search for God's Messenger" must be made. Here, intellect starts investigating the people who claimed that they received God's message and are His Messengers. Now, intelligence critically assesses and investigates these claimants and their message.

In this regard, the intellect tests the life of the messenger and his message according to two parameters: first, Historical Credibility, second, Harmony between God's message and human nature, because God is the Creator of man as well as the Giver of the message, so no contradiction must be found therein.

After thorough investigation, human intelligence reaches the sixth and final conclusion that now it must "follow the message of God given by the Messenger" without any further questioning or doubt, i.e., total obedience.

Trap of Example

"Allah puts forth a similitude: a (slave) man belonging to many partners (like those who worship others along with Allah) disputing with one another, and a (slave) man belonging entirely to one master (like those who worship Allah Alone). Are those two equal in comparison?"(113)

Supporting or explaining a hypothesis with the aid of an example is common practice. It lends meaning to the hypothesis as it is considered a proof of thinking and knowledge. Examples play a very significant role in convincing the readers of the subject matter. However, an example may guide as well as misguide us. A critical analysis of the given example is rarely undertaken. Generally, readers are less conscious and rather careless about the critical scrutiny of the examples. Particularly in the field of religion, wrong examples can easily push a person on the wrong track. As a result, his complete approach and attitude gets corrupted even without him realizing it.

Religion is a very important part of life, if not the most important. Our total behavior, individual and social, is governed by our religion. We may say that our religious tendencies fix our world-view. Consequently, wrong thoughts and perspective inevitably lead to wrong action. Thus, the critical assessment of thoughts should be accorded a very special place in our mental drill. Otherwise, we may easily be trapped. The following instances will be helpful to understand the misguidance of innocent people by way of misconstrued examples:

- Referring to the idols of deities, most of the polytheist state - "If you believe; it is God, if you don't believe; it is stone." But, when we critical analyze this example, we find that this is not a question of believing or not believing at all. If believing could change the reality, then we might have considered it. But it is a well-established fact that merely our belief can never convert tea into coffee. Thus, this example is wrong. Rather, the right thing is to find out the reality in definite terms - whether it is stone or God.

- The Christians believe in the concept of Trinity i.e., God, Son of God and Holy Spirit. They say 'one in three' and 'three in one', like water, which can be solid, liquid and gas. Again, this is a wrong example, because water - be it in the form of solid (ice), liquid or gas (vapor) – comprises of the same constituent in each state i.e., H_2O. But in the stated concept of Trinity, the above –mentioned three personalities are totally different. Otherwise, after the Crucifixion, God and the Holy Spirit would also have died. Also, according to the Bible, Jesus Christ ate food, drank water, slept and felt tired, but God and the Holy Spirit never did or experienced such things.

- Some people proclaim that since God is merciful, why should He condemn the criminals to hell? Rather, He should forgive all. However, after a careful study, we see that this is a wrong approach to view this situation. Very few people can differentiate between a right frame of reference and a wrong frame of reference. This action of God would be wrong when our reference point is 'Mercy', but in order to reach a reasonable conclusion it should rather be seen from the point of view of 'Justice' and not 'Mercy'. Justice is, in fact, the result of mercy.

- Some people, namely those who advocate and support the wrong concept of an intermediary between God and Man, often give this example - "If you want to meet the Prime Minister, you first ought to go and meet his Personal Assistant. Or, if you want to reach the rooftop of a building, you will have to use a ladder or the lift of the building. Therefore, reaching God is not possible except through an intermediary like a 'peer' (a spiritual guide) or a priest, a pundit or a guru etc.

This example is wrong in its very application. That's because, there is a distance and a gap between you and the P.M., he does not know anything about you. Also, there is a physical distance between you, being on the ground floor, and the rooftop. But, there is no distance between God and man. God is very close to you and always with you. He is well acquainted with all your thoughts, feelings and actions; even better than you are with your own self.

God-centered life v/s Man-centered life

"I (Allah) have not created the Jinn and the men
except that they should serve Me".(114)

When a person accepts God as his Mabud (Lord), he
voluntarily becomes his Abd (Slave) in faith and deeds and his
whole life willingly turns into that of Ibadat (Slavery). Ibadat,
in essence, means a God- centered life or God-oriented life -
A life which is very easy to lead for the one who has turned to
God in sincerity and repentance. We may say that there are
two approaches towards leading a human life:

* **God-centered life**

* **Man-centered life**

When, before the performance of any action or deed, one
takes into consideration the Will of God, the limits set down
by Him and the ways most pleasing to Him, then he can
really leading a 'God-centered life.' On the contrary, giving
preference to the choice of man (e.g., self, relatives, friends,
neighbors and society) in all activities of life may be termed
as 'Man-centered life.'

The orientations of these two approaches are contradictory
in their very nature. It is absolutely impossible to please both
God and human being in all our actions. But, there can be

certain actions that please God and Man at the same time. For instance, the virtues of good behavior with parents, to be honest in labor etc. are appreciated and encouraged by both.

But, pleasing every man all the time is not possible. You might please one and consequently displease another or you might please a man by carrying out one action according to his like but refusal to do anymore will obviously displease him.

The Prophet Muhammad said:

"When a person wants to please God without considering the people's likes or dislikes, God makes him carefree from the people. And when a person wants to please people to displease God, He hands him to the people's (disposal)". (115)

Noticeably, it is very easy to please one God than to attempt the satisfaction of all human beings. Generally it may be observed that a person might get ninety-nine of his demands were met but resents the non-fulfillment of a mere one task. Quite the opposite, true repentance and sincere askance of pardon pleases God easily.

Infact, it might be safely said that a man who manages to make everyone happy by fulfilling all of their demands must be corrupt. He cannot be genuine. This is because different people have different demands - right as well as wrong – and they cannot be happy until and unless all their demands, good or bad, are met. The praise of a person who carries out all of the people's expectations, moral or immoral, is a proof that he is also committing wrong deeds. Thus we may conclude that leading a perfect Man-centered life is not a possibility.

But let's take the example of a man who makes earning the pleasure of God his only aim of his life. Now, God helps him in a way, which is absolutely beyond his sketch of imagination and calculation. On the contrary, a person who wastes all his efforts to earn the pleasure of man, God leaves him on the mercy of people itself. Such a person loses from all sides as he neither gets freedom from the slavery of people, nor is he able to please them completely.

Thus, it is much more difficult and rather worthless to spend a Man-centered life than God-centered life. It is impossible to please all the people, all the time. The following story beautifully expresses the nature of majority of the people:

There was an old man who always preferred God's Pleasure to Man's pleasure. His young son disliked this habit of his father and always criticized him on this head. His own behavior was people-oriented. The old man, in order to explain his point of view to his son, accompanied him on a journey.

The old man took a donkey and told his son to ride on it but walked on foot himself. As they passed through the inhabitants of an area, the people commented, "See! What a cruel son! He is himself riding the donkey, whereas his old father is walking on foot". Listening to this, the son got down and his father rode the donkey.

Traveling further, they passed through another area whose inhabitants now exclaimed: "Look! What a selfish father! He is himself riding the donkey, but his young son is walking on foot". The son took note of it and sat on the donkey too.

But, when crossed through another locality, the people said, "What cruel people! They are doing injustice to an innocent, weak animal". The son again heeded to the people and thus both got down the donkey and walked by foot. They reached another city. The inhabitants saw them and said, "What foolish people they are! They have an animal but are walking on foot!"

Human Life in Past, Present and Future

Perspective from the Quran

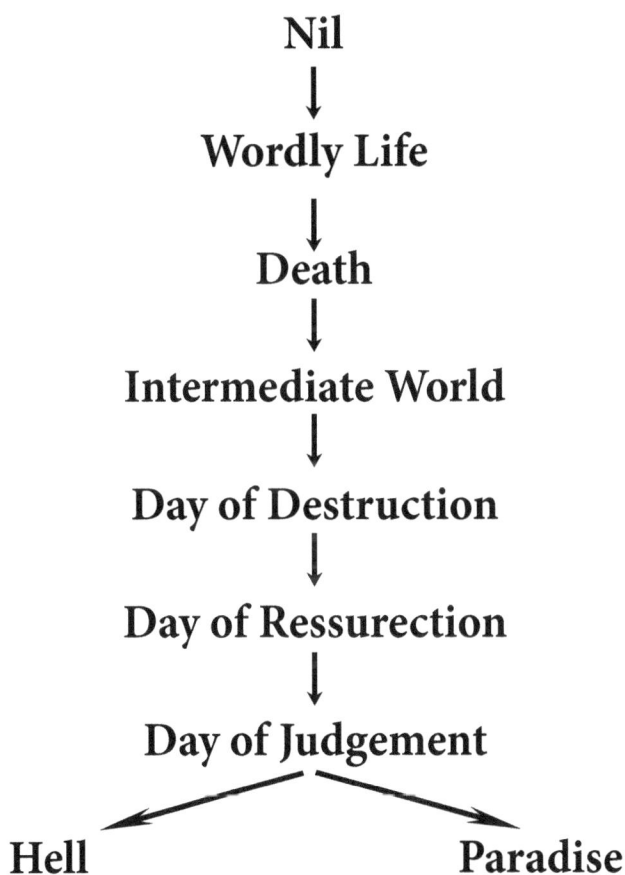

Nil
↓
Wordly Life
↓
Death
↓
Intermediate World
↓
Day of Destruction
↓
Day of Ressurection
↓
Day of Judgement

Hell ← → **Paradise**

Human life, according to the Quran, goes through the following stages:

Nil

Has there not been over Man a long period of Time, when he was nothing - (not even) mentioned? (116)

Worldly Life

He Who created Death and Life, that He may try which of you is best in deed. (117)

The life of this world is but goods and chattels of deception. (118)

Death

Every soul shall have a taste of death. (119)

Intermediate World

(After death) Before them is a Partition till the Day they are raised up. (120)

Day of Destruction

Assuredly, what ye are promised must come to pass. Then when the stars become dim; when the heaven is cleft asunder; When the mountains are scattered (to the winds) as dust. (121)

Day of Resurrection

In the end to Us shall ye brought back.(122)

Then when the Trumpet is blown, there will be no more relationships between them that Day, nor will one ask after another. (123)

It will be on a Day when He will call you, and ye will answer (His call) with (words of) His praise, and ye will think that ye tarried but a little while. (124)

The Day whereon they will issue from their sepulchers in sudden haste as if they were rushing to a goal-post (fixed for them), - Their eyes lowered in dejection, - ignominy covering them (all over)! Such is the Day the which they are promised. (125)

One day He will gather them together: (It will be) as if they had tarried but an hour of a day: they will recognise each other: assuredly those will be lost who denied the meeting with Allah and refused to receive true guidance. (126)

Day of Judgment

(Allah) Master of the Day of Judgment. (127)

Only on the Day of Judgment shall you be paid your full recompense.(128)

Every man's fate We have fastened on his own neck: On the Day of Judgment We shall bring out for him a scroll, which he will see spread open. (It will be said to him:) Read thine (own) record: Sufficient is thy soul this day to make out an account against thee. (129)

Anyone who has done an atom's weight of good, see it! And anyone who has done an atom's weight of evil, shall see it. (130)

That Day shall We set a seal on their mouths. But their hands will speak to us, and their feet bear witness, to all that they did. (131)

On the Day that the enemies of Allah will be gathered together to the Fire, they will be marched in ranks.At length, when they reach the (Fire), their hearing, their sight, and their skins will bear witness against them, as to (all) their deeds. They will say to their skins: "Why bear ye witness against us?" They will say: "(Allah) hath given us speech, - (He) Who giveth speech to everything: He created you for the first time, and unto Him were ye to return. Ye did not seek to hide yourselves, lest your hearing, your sight, and your skins should bear witness against you! But ye did think that Allah knew not many of the things that ye used to do! But this thought of yours which ye did entertain concerning your Lord, hath brought you to destruction, and (now) have ye become of those utterly lost. (132)

Then those whose balance (of good deeds) is heavy, - they will attain salvation: But those whose balance is light, will be those who have lost their souls, in Hell will they abide. (133)

Friends on that day will be foes, one to another, - except the Righteous. (134)

Some faces, that Day, will beam (in brightness and beauty); - Looking towards their Lord; And some faces, that Day, will be sad and dismal, In the thought that some back-breaking calamity was about to be inflicted on them. (135)

Verily, from (the Light of) their Lord, that Day, will they (disbelievers) be veiled. (136)

Hell

For those who reject their Lord (and Cherisher) is the Penalty of Hell: and evil is (such), Destination. (137)

Those who reject our Signs, We shall soon cast into the Fire: as often as their skins are roasted through, We shall change them for fresh skins, that they may taste the penalty. (138)

For the wrong-doers We have prepared a Fire whose (smoke and flames), like the walls and roof of a tent, will hem them in: if they implore relief they will be granted water like melted brass, that will scald their faces, how dreadful the drink! How uncomfortable a couch to recline on. (139)

These two antagonists dispute with each other about their Lord: But those who deny (their Lord), - for them will be cut out a garment of Fire: over their heads will be poured out boiling water. With it will be scalded what is within their bodies, as well as (their) skins. In addition there will be maces of iron (to punish) them. Every time they wish to get away there from, from anguish, they will be forced back therein, and (it will be said), "Taste ye the Penalty of Burning!(140)

For it is a tree that springs out of the bottom of Hell-Fire: The shoots of its fruit-stalks are like the heads of devils: Truly they will eat thereof and fill their bellies therewith. Then on top of that they will be given a mixture made of boiling water. (141)

(They) Shall dwell for ever in the Fire, and be given, to drink, boiling water, so that it cuts up their bowels (to pieces). (142)

Those who reject the Book and the (revelations) with which We sent our apostles: but soon shall they know, - When the yokes (shall be) round their necks, and the chains; they shall be dragged along- In the boiling fetid fluid: then in the Fire shall they be burned; Then shall it be said to them: "Where are the (deities) to which ye gave part- worship- In derogation of Allah." They will reply: "They have left us in the lurch: Nay, we invoked not, of old, anything (that had real existence)." Thus does Allah leave the Unbelievers to stray. That was because ye were wont to rejoice on the earth in things other than the Truth, and that ye were wont to be insolent. Enter ye the gates of Hell, to dwell therein: and evil is (this) abode of the arrogant. (143)

Truly Hell is as a place of ambush, For the transgressors a place of destination: They will dwell therein for ages. Nothing cool shall they taste therein, nor any drink, Save a boiling fluid and a fluid, dark, murky, intensely cold, A fitting recompense (for them). For that they used not to fear any account (for their deeds), But they (impudently) treated Our Signs as false. (144)

They shall have Layers of Fire above them, and Layers (of Fire) below them. (145)

Paradise

Only he who is saved far from the Fire and admitted to the Garden will have attained the object (of Life): (146)

As to those who believe and work righteous deeds, they have, for their entertainment, the Gardens of Paradise, Wherein they shall dwell (for aye): no change will they wish for from them. (147)

For them will be Gardens of Eternity; beneath them rivers

will flow; they will be adorned therein with bracelets of gold, and they will wear green garments of fine silk and heavy brocade: They will recline therein on raised thrones. How good the recompense! How beautiful a couch to recline on! (148)

Verily the Companions of the Garden shall that Day have joy in all that they do; They and their associates will be in groves of (cool) shade, reclining on Thrones (of dignity); (Every) fruit (enjoyment) will be there for them; they shall have whatever they call for; "Peace!" - a word (of salutation) from a Lord Most Merciful. (149)

Among Gardens and Springs; Dressed in fine silk and in rich brocade, they will face each other; So; and We shall join them to Companions with beautiful, big, and lustrous eyes. There can they call for every kind of fruit in peace and security; Nor will they there taste Death, except the first death; and He will preserve them from the Penalty of the Blazing Fire, - (150)

(Here is) a Parable of the Garden which the righteous are promised: in it are rivers of water incorruptible; rivers of milk of which the taste never changes; rivers of wine, a joy to those who drink; and rivers of honey pure and clear. In it there are for them all kinds of fruits; and Grace from their Lord. (151)

Reclining in the (Garden) on raised thrones, they will see there neither the sun's (excessive heat) nor (the moon's) excessive cold. And the shades of the (Garden) will come low over them, and the bunches (of fruit), there, will hang low in humility. And amongst them will be passed round vessels of silver and goblets of crystal, - Crystal-clear, made of silver: they will determine the measure thereof (according to their wishes). And they will be given to drink there of a

Cup (of Wine) mixed with Zanjabil, - A fountain there, called Salsabil. And round about them will (serve) youths of perpetual (freshness): If thou seest them, thou wouldst think them scattered Pearls. And when thou lookest, it is there thou wilt see a Bliss and a Realm Magnificent. Upon them will be green Garments of fine silk and heavy brocade, and they will be adorned with Bracelets of silver; and their Lord will give to them to drink of a Wine Pure and Holy. Verily this is a Reward for you, and your Endeavour is accepted and recognised. (152)

Ye shall have therein abundance of fruit, from which ye shall have satisfaction.(153)

Verily for the Righteous there will be a fulfillment of (the heart's) desires; Gardens enclosed, and grapevines; Companions of equal age; And a cup full (to the brim). No vanity shall they hear therein, nor Untruth. (154)

But give glad tidings to those who believe and work righteousness, that their portion is Gardens, beneath which rivers flow. Every time they are fed with fruits there from, they say: Why, this is what we were fed with before, for they are given things in similitude; and they have therein companions pure (and holy); and they abide therein (for ever). (155)

(Being) those who have believed in Our Signs and bowed (their wills to Ours) in Islam. Enter ye the Garden, ye and your wives, in (beauty and) rejoicing. To them will be passed round, dishes and goblets of gold: there will be there all that the souls could desire, all that their eyes could delight in: and ye shall abide therein (for aye). Such will be the Garden of which ye are made heirs for your (good) deeds (in life). (156)

Equality and Inequality

A Quranic approach

The condition of being alike in status and rights is termed as 'equality'. On the other hand, an unfair difference or absence of identical comparison may be understood as 'inequality'.

The existence of inequality in deeds that are out of human control cannot be taken as a criterion to establish superiority or inferiority. It can rather be understood as "difference" and, in essence, is the beauty of life. Inequality has both permanent and temporary causes.

The differences in family, race, color, caste, language, nation and profession are considered permanent reasons of inequality. Whereas, the dissimilarities of wealth, children, power, beauty, knowledge, expertise, culture and creed are its temporary causes.

The Quran is guidance given by The Creator for all of mankind. Therefore, it naturally follows that it would represent a perfect combination explaining diversity as well as equality.

The Qur'anic concept of equality is as follows:

The origin of all mankind traced to a single man

"O mankind! We created you from a single (pair) of a male and a female, and made you into nations and tribes, that ye may know each other (not that ye may despise (each other). Verily the most honoured of you in the sight of Allah is (he who is) the most righteous of you. And Allah has full knowledge and is well acquainted (with all things)". (157)

"He created you (all) from a single person: then created, of like nature, his mate; and he sent down for you eight herd of cattle in pairs: He makes you, in the wombs of your mothers, in stages, one after another, in three veils of darkness. Such is Allah, your Lord and Cherisher: to Him belongs dominion. There is no god but He: then how are ye turned away". (158)

"O mankind! Revere your Guardian-Lord, who created you from a single person, created, of like nature, His mate, and from them twain scattered (like seeds) countless men and women; revere Allah, through whom ye demand your mutual (rights), and (revere) the wombs (That bore you): for Allah ever watches over you". (159)

"It is He Who hath produced you from a single person: here is a place of sojourn and a place of departure: We detail Our signs for people who understand."(160)

Similar composition of every man:

"And Allah did create you from dust; then from a sperm-drop; then He made you in pairs. And no female conceives, or lays down (her load), but with His knowledge. Nor is a man long-lived granted length of days, nor is a part cut off from his life, but is in a Decree (ordained). All this is easy to Allah. (161)

"It is He Who has created you from dust then from a sperm-drop, then from a leech-like clot; then does he get you out (into the light) as a child: then lets you (grow and) reach your age of full strength; then lets you become old, though of you there are some who die before; and lets you reach a Term appointed; in order that ye may learn wisdom."(162)

"O mankind! If ye have a doubt about the Resurrection, (consider) that We created you out of dust, then out of sperm, then out of a leech-like clot, then out of a morsel of flesh, partly formed and partly unformed, in order that We may manifest (our power) to you; and We cause whom We will to rest in the wombs for an appointed term, then do We bring you out as babes, then (foster you) that ye may reach your age of full strength; and some of you are called to die, and some are sent back to the feeblest old age, so that they know nothing after having known (much), and (further), thou seest the earth barren and lifeless, but when We pour down rain on it, it is stirred (to life), it swells, and it puts forth every kind of beautiful growth (in pairs)". (163)

The Creator's same concern for all of mankind:

" Verily, We created man in the best stature (mould)".(164)

" Allah, it is He who has made for you the earth as a dwelling place and the sky as a canopy, and has given you shape and made your shapes good (looking) and has provided you with good things". (165)

" O man! What has made you careless about your Lord, the Most Generous? Who created you, fashioned you perfectly, and gave you due proportion." (166)

Identical aim of life:

" I (Allah) created not the Jinn and mankind except that they should worship Me (alone)". (167)

Every man deserves same respect:

"He (Satan) said: "Seest Thou? This is the one whom Thou hast honoured above me! If Thou wilt but respite me to the Day of Judgment, I will surely bring his descendants under my sway - all but a few! ((Allah)) said: Go thy way; if any of them follow thee, verily Hell will be the recompense of you (all)- an ample recompense.Lead to destruction those whom thou canst among them, with thy (seductive) voice; make assaults on them with thy cavalry and thy infantry; mutually share with them wealth and children; and make promises to them." But Satan promises them nothing but deceit. As for My servants, no authority shalt thou have over them:" Enough is thy Lord for a Disposer of affairs.Your Lord is He that maketh the Ship go smoothly for you through the sea, in order that ye may seek of his Bounty. For he is unto you most Merciful. When distress seizes you at sea, those that ye call upon - besides Himself - leave you in the lurch! But when He brings you back safe to land, ye turn away (from Him). Most ungrateful is man! Do ye then feel secure that He will not cause you to be swallowed up beneath the earth when ye are on land, or that He will not send against you a violent tornado (with showers of stones) so that ye shall find no one to carry out your affairs for you?

Or do ye feel secure that He will not send you back a second time to sea and send against you a heavy gale to drown you because of your ingratitude, so that ye find no helper.

Therein against Us? We have honoured the sons of Adam; provided them with transport on land and sea; given them for sustenance things good and pure; and conferred on them special favours, above a great part of our creation". (168)

Every man bestowed with same level of intelligence at first:

"Nor take life - which Allah has made sacred - except for just cause. And if anyone is slain wrongfully, we have given his heir authority (to demand qisas or to forgive): but let him nor exceed bounds in the matter of taking life; for he is helped". (169)

The elements of inequality from the Qur'anic point of view are as follows:

Inevitable difference between a believer and a disbeliever:

"Is then the man who believes no better than the man who is rebellious and wicked? Not equal are they. For those who believe and do righteous deeds are Gardens as hospitable homes, for their (good) deeds. As to those who are rebellious and wicked, their abode will be the Fire: every time they wish to get away there from, they will be forced there into, and it will be said to them: Taste ye the Penalty of the Fire, the which ye were wont to reject as false".(170)

Dwellers of Paradise and Hell / Believer and Disbeliever in the Hereafter:

"Not equal are the Companions of the Fire and the Companions of the Garden: it is the Companions of the

Garden, that will achieve Felicity".(171)

" The (material) things which ye are given are but the conveniences of this life and the glitter thereof; but that which is with Allah is better and more enduring: will ye not then be wise? Are (these two) alike? - one to whom We have made a goodly promise, and who is going to reach its (fulfillment), and one to whom We have given the good things of this life, but who, on the Day of Judgment, is to be among those brought up (for punishment)? (172)

The struggler and non-struggler in the way of Allah:

"Not equal are those believers who sit (at home) and receive no hurt, and those who strive and fight in the cause of Allah with their goods and their persons. Allah hath granted a grade higher to those who strive and fight with their goods and persons than to those who sit (at home). Unto all (in Faith) Hath Allah promised good: But those who strive and fight Hath He distinguished above those who sit (at home) by a special reward,- Ranks specially bestowed by Him, and Forgiveness and Mercy. For Allah is Oft-forgiving, Most Merciful". (173)

"Do ye make the giving of drink to pilgrims, or the maintenance of the Sacred Mosque, equal to (the pious service of) those who believe in Allah and the Last Day, and strive with might and main in the cause of Allah. They are not comparable in the sight of Allah. and Allah guides not those who do wrong. Those who believe, and suffer exile and strive with might and main, in Allah's cause, with their goods and their persons, have the highest rank in the sight of Allah. They are the people who will achieve (salvation)". (174)

A charitable man and an uncharitable one:

"And what cause have ye why ye should not spend in the cause of Allah.- For to Allah belongs the heritage of the heavens and the earth. Not equal among you are those who spent (freely) and fought, before the Victory, (with those who did so later). Those are higher in rank than those who spent (freely) and fought afterwards. But to all has Allah promised a goodly (reward). And Allah is well acquainted with all that ye do". (175)

A useful member of society and a useless one:

"Allah sets forth the Parable (of two men: one) a slave under the dominion of another; He has no power of any sort; and (the other) a man on whom We have bestowed goodly favours from Ourselves, and he spends thereof (freely), privately and publicly: are the two equal? (By no means;) praise be to Allah. But most of them understand not. Allah sets forth (another) Parable of two men: one of them dumb, with no power of any sort; a wearisome burden is he to his master; whichever way be directs him, he brings no good: is such a man equal with one who commands Justice, and is on a Straight Way? " (176)

God-fearer and one who does not fear God:

"When some trouble toucheth man, he crieth unto his Lord, turning to Him in repentance: but when He bestoweth a favour upon him as from Himself, (man) doth forget what he cried and prayed for before, and he doth set up rivals unto Allah, thus misleading others from Allah.s Path. Say: Enjoy thy blasphemy for a little while: verily thou art (one) of the Companions of the Fire!Is one who worships devoutly during the hour of the night prostrating himself or standing (in adoration), who takes heed of the Hereafter, and who places his hope in the Mercy of his Lord - (like one who does not)? Say: Are those equal, those who know and those who do not know? It is those who are endued with understanding that receive admonition". (177)

Good deeds and evil deeds:

"Not equal are the blind and those who (clearly) see: Nor are (equal) those who believe and work deeds of righteousness, and those who do evil. Little do ye learn by admonition! The Hour will certainly come: Therein is no doubt: Yet most men believe not". (178)

Right beliefs coupled with good deeds and wrong beliefs coupled with evil:

"Who doth more wrong than those who invent a life against Allah. They will be turned back to the presence of their Lord, and the witnesses will say, "These are the ones who lied against their Lord! Behold! The Curse of Allah is on those who do wrong! Those who would hinder (men) from the path of Allah and would seek in it something crooked: these were they who denied the Hereafter! They will in no wise frustrate (His design) on earth, nor have they protectors besides Allah. Their penalty will be doubled! They lost the power to hear, and they did not see! They are the ones who have lost their own souls: and the (fancies) they invented have left them in the lurch! Without a doubt, these are the very ones who will lose most in the Hereafter!

But those who believe and work righteousness, and humble

themselves before their Lord,- They will be companions of the gardens, to dwell therein for aye! These two kinds (of men) may be compared to the blind and deaf, and those who can see and hear well. Are they equal when compared? Will ye not then take heed? " (179)

Monotheism and Polytheism:

"Say: Who is the Lord and Sustainer of the heavens and the earth? Say:(It is) Allah. Say: "Do ye then take (for worship) protectors other than Him, such as have no power either for good or for harm to themselves? Say: Are the blind equal with those who see? Or the depths of darkness equal with light? Or do they assign to Allah partners who have created (anything) as He has created, so that the creation seemed to them similar? Say:(Allah) is the Creator of all things: He is the One, the Supreme and Irresistible". (180)

A thinker and a non-thinker:

"We send the apostles only to give good news and to warn: so those who believe and mend (their lives),- upon them shall be no fear, nor shall they grieve. But those who reject our signs, them shall punishment touch, for that they ceased not from transgressing. Say: I tell you not that with me are the treasures of Allah, nor do I know what is hidden, nor do I tell you I am an angel. I but follow what is revealed to me. Say: can the blind be held equal to the seeing? Will ye then consider not? "(181)

" The blind and the seeing are not alike; Nor are the depths of Darkness and the Light; Nor are the (chilly) shade and the (genial) heat of the sun: Nor are alike those that are living and those that are dead. Allah can make any that He wills to hear; but thou canst not make those to hear who are (buried) in graves". (182)

Soft-hearted and Hard-hearted man

"Seest thou not that Allah sends down rain from the sky, and leads it through springs in the earth? Then He causes to grow, therewith, produce of various colours: then it withers; thou wilt see it grow yellow; then He makes it dry up and crumble away. Truly, in this, is a Message of remembrance to men of understanding. Is one whose heart Allah has opened to Islam, so that he has received Enlightenment from Allah, (no better than one hard-hearted)? Woe to those whose hearts are hardened against celebrating the praises of Allah. they are manifestly wandering (in error)!" (183)

Faith and knowledge

"O ye who believe! When ye are told to make room in the assemblies, (spread out and) make room: (ample) room will Allah provide for you. And when ye are told to rise up, rise up Allah will rise up, to (suitable) ranks (and degrees), those of you who believe and who have been granted (mystic) Knowledge. And Allah is well- acquainted with all ye do". (184)

According to the Qur'an, the differences among human beings are for the sake of identity and are not to be considered as the criterion of superiority or inferiority. The only thing which is the yardstick of real difference i.e. superiority or inferiority is "piety".

"O mankind! We created you from a single (pair) of a male

and a female, and made you into nations and tribes, that ye may know each other (not that ye may despise (each other). Verily the most honoured of you in the sight of Allah is (he who is) the most righteous of you. And Allah has full knowledge and is well acquainted (with all things)". (185)

It must be noted here that the economic disparity among people is the root cause for promotion of cooperation and competition amongst them.

"they say: "Why is not this Qur'an sent down to some leading man in either of the two (chief) cities? Is it they who would portion out the Mercy of thy Lord? It is We Who portion out between them their livelihood in the life of this world: and We raise some of them above others in ranks, so that some may command work from others. But the Mercy of thy Lord is better than the (wealth) which they amass". (186)

The elevated financial status of a person is not for the purpose of according him respect and neither is the lack thereof, a means to insult. Had everyone been created rich, no one would have offered his/her services to the other less fortunate.

If we are realistic in our assessment, then we would all agree that this monetary dissimilarity is not permanent but rather temporary in nature. A servant may change and elevate his financial status by using the correct means coupled with hard work and smartness. In fact, it is not impossible to imagine a scenario where he might be able to hire his own master! The dignity of work is the basic teaching of the Qur'an.

We should not be deceived by this kind of difference. Rather view I in its correct perspective i.e. it is only for test and trial of man. Both, richness and poverty are an examination. The rich is tested in the usage of his wealth and the poor in his patience.

"And the apostles whom We sent before thee were all (men) who ate food and walked through the streets: We have made some of you as a trial for others: will ye have patience? for Allah is One Who sees (all things)". (187)

That is why the Holy Qur'an says:

"And in no wise covet those things in which Allah Hath bestowed His gifts More freely on some of you than on others: To men is allotted what they earn, and to women what they earn: But ask Allah of His bounty. For Allah hath full knowledge of all things". (188)

Half Truth

Most of the times, religious speeches and writings merely address half or incomplete teachings of religion, be it intentionally or unintentionally. The remaining half of the truth of a teaching and the incomplete information further confuses people and they find themselves unable to correctly or systematically implement that teaching in their life.

With particular reference to the sphere of Islam, we often observe the following teachings being propagated, but only in a limited context i.e. half and incomplete –

Guidance of Allah:

Majority of Islamic writers and speakers discuss that God Guides. This fact is clearly stated in the Qur'an. But they do not ascertain as to upon whom is this guidance Bestowed. The Holy Qur'an clearly lays out the answer -

"(Allah) Guides whom He wills". (189)

"(Allah) Guides to Himself those who turns (to Him) in repentance and in obedience". (190)

Acceptance of repentance:

Most people involved in teaching Islam highlight that God Forgives and Accepts repentance but they don't explain who

God Forgives and whom He does not.

"Allah accept the repentance of those who do evil in ignorance and repent soon afterwards; to them will Allah turn in mercy: For Allah is full of knowledge and wisdom. Of no effect is the repentance of those who continue to do evil, until death faces one of them, and he says, "Now have I repented indeed;" nor of those who die rejecting Faith: for them have We prepared a punishment most grievous". (191)

Seeking assistance of Allah:

In the face of problems, we are often advised and told to seek help from Allah. But, it is rarely made clear how this assistance should be sought. However, we don't have to go very far for the answer. The Qur'an has already addressed this issue.

"O ye who believe! seek help with patient perseverance and prayer; for Allah is with those who patiently persevere".(192)

"Nay, seek ((Allah)'s) help with patient perseverance and prayer: It is indeed hard, except to those who bring a lowly spirit". (193)

"Do no mischief on the earth, after it hath been set in order, but call on Him with fear and longing (in your hearts): for the Mercy of Allah is (always) near to those who do good". (194)

Trust in Allah:

The concept of having complete trust in Allah is well-preached and much taught. Even the Qur'an states:

"Say: Nothing will happen to us except what Allah has decreed forus: He is our protector": and on Allah let the Believers put their trust". (195)

"Lo! The hypocrites say, and those in whose hearts is a disease: These people,- their religion has misled them. But if any trust in Allah, behold! Allah is Exalted in might, Wise". (196)

Every writer, orator and speaker advances this concept to all people: those in distress or otherwise. But, very few actually answer as to what 'trust in Allah' actually means, what is the means to acquire that trust and how is it manifested. However, the following ahadith make it very clear –

Hazrat Anas narrated - "One day Prophet Muhammad, noticed a Bedouin leaving his camel without tying it and he asked the Bedouin, "Why don't you tie down your camel?" The Bedouin answered, "I put my trust in Allah." The Prophet then said, "Tie your camel first, and then put your trust in Allah." (197)

Narrated Hazrat Umar: I heard the Prophet who was saying, "If you (human beings) keep trust in God with full certainty, He will Give you your livelihood as He Gives the sparrows (their livelihood). The sparrows come out from their nests with empty stomach but return in the evening with filled bellies." (198)

Spending for Allah's pleasure:

It is often discussed that Allah is pleased when we spend our wealth and money for a good cause. The following verse of the Quran explains this concept –

"It is not required of thee (O Messenger, to set them on the right path, but Allah sets on the right path whom He pleaseth. Whatever of good ye give benefits your own souls, and ye shall only do so seeking the "Face" of Allah. Whatever good ye give, shall be rendered back to you, and ye shall not be dealt with unjustly". (199)

But, in what limits should this money be spent to seek God's pleasure and in what way, is seldom mentioned. This is despite the fact that Allah, Himself, states in the Qur'an –

"Those who, when they spend, are not extravagant and not niggardly, but hold a just (balance) between those (extremes)". (200)

"And render to the kindred their due rights, as (also) to those in want, and to the wayfarer: But squander not (your wealth) in the manner of a spendthrift". (201)

Remembrance of Allah:

Also, many people always instruct us to only call upon God and remember Him in all circumstances. Allah says in the Quran –

"Then do ye remember Me; I will remember you. Be grateful to Me, and reject not Faith". (202)

But, the correct way to call upon Allah and to remember Him is not often explained and given its due right. This point is extremely crucial, as it is imperative that man only calls upon God as He wants us to, otherwise there is grave danger of unknowingly associating partners with Allah and innovating in our Deen. The Qur'an unfailingly addresses this important issue –

"Do no mischief on the earth, after it hath been set in order, but call on Him with fear and longing (in your hearts): for the Mercy of Allah is (always) near to those who do good". (203)

The case of oaths and covenants:

Oaths and covenants are not to be taken as mere play and amusement. The promises and oaths that come out of the mouth of a Muslim hold immense value. They, if once pronounced, are to be fulfilled with utmost sincerity. Everyone will be questioned about his or her oaths and covenants. This Qur'anic teaching is repeatedly pronounced –

"Fulfil the Covenant of Allah when ye have entered into it, and break not your oaths after ye have confirmed them; indeed ye have made Allah your surety; for Allah knoweth all that ye do". (204)

It is clear that breaking oaths and covenants is a punishable offence, a sin. But, without letting our imagination run away with us, we have to ponder on the question – What kind of oaths come under this category and maybe liable for punishment? And – is there any way by which we may compensate for breaking the same? These important questions are not made clear without the questioner actually asking explicitly. However, undoubtedly, the Quran addresses each and every issue of vitality –

"Allah will not call you to account for what is futile in your oaths, but He will call you to account for your deliberate oaths: for expiation, feed ten indigent persons, on a scale of the average for the food of your families; or clothe them; or give a slave his freedom. If that is beyond your means, fast for

Obey one, communicate yours and respect all

three days. That is the expiation for the oaths ye have sworn. But keep to your oaths. Thus doth Allah make clear to you His signs, that ye may be grateful". (205)

References

(1) Quran: chapter no.15, verse no.9

(2) Quran, 3:19

(3) Quran, 3:85

(4) Quran, 2:185

(5) Quran, 10:57

(6) Quran, 45:20

(7) Quran, 15:19

(8) Quran, 54:17

(9) Quran, 21:10

(10) Quran, 14:2

(11) Quran, 24:52

(12) Quran, 16:97

(13) Quran, 10:57-58

(14) In fact all religions of today are not one but different. But the similarities in many of their teachings (e.g.,all religions like truth and condemn lies, each one encourages honesty

and denounces dishonesty, each and every one prohibits contradiction of words and deeds, everyone is a supporter of justice and peace etc.) are found because the source of all revealed religions is one i.e., God.

Today, some element of truth is found in all religions due to their common source. However the ratio of truth varies from religion to religion e.g., some have 20% truth, some 40% or 60% etc. Obviously, man should accept such a religion which guarantees 100% truth.

A formula for accessing the degree of truthfulness of any religion is to check any religious claim from two aspects:

First, "Historical Credibility" means the message of God must be available today in its original language and content.

Second, "Harmony with Human Nature" - the message of God must be harmonious with and not contradictory to human nature or human composition, because the Creator of man and Giver of religion is one (God).

(15) Quran, 42:13

(16) The term 'Islam' is applicable in two different meaning as regards to its origin:

Firstly, Adam - the first man and first Prophet of God - presented a religion named Islam.

Secondly, the religion that was presented by Prophet Muhammad is also Islam. Infact, no man is the founder of Islam but God.

Islam is based on the guidance of God for whole mankind. Every Prophet of God presented the same religion that was

Islam.

And Islam presented by Muhammad is the last and preserved form of all previous messages brought by all messengers of God.

According to the Quran, after the coming of Prophet Muhammad, Allah will not accept any other religion in life hereafter, but before him, the religions presented by all the true Prophets will be accepted, because they were all from God.

(17) Quran, 3:52

(18) Quran, 7:68

(19) Quran, 3:19 / 5:3

(20) Quran, 3:85

(21) Quran, 3:104

(22) Quran, 3:114

(23) Quran, 3:110

(24) Quran, 22:67

(25) Quran, 41:33

(26) Quran, 9:71,112 / 22:41

(27) Quran, 16:125

(28) Quran, 20:44 / 3:159

(29) Quran, 41:34 / 23:96

(30) Quran, 16:125 / 29:46

(31) Quran, 6:108

(32) Quran, 22:67-69

(33) Quran, 3:64

(34) Quran, 26:214 / 6:74

(35) Quran, 2:256 / 25:57 / 73:19 / 74:55 / 76:29

(36) Quran, 109:6

(37) Quran, 6:108

(38) Quran, 41:53

(39) Quran, 4:56

(40) Quran, 21:30

(41) Quran, 51:49

(42) Quran, 36:36

(43) Quran, 21:30

(44) Quran, 36:82

(45) Quran, 41:11

(46) Quran, 71:16 / 10:5

(47) Quran, 36:38

(48) Quran, 21:33

(49) Quran, 21:44 / 13:41

(50) Quran, 78:6-7

(51) Quran, 27:88

(52) Quran, 13:12

(53) Quran, 6:125

(54) Quran, 4:34

(55) Quran, 2:236

(56) Quran, 36:82

(57) Quran, 50:38

(58) Quran, 15:9

(59) Quran, 3:49/1:6

(60) The book of Matthew, 15:24

(61) Quran, 56:79

(62) Quran, 2:185

(63) Quran, 14:2

(64) Quran, 85:21-22

(65) Quran, 3:28

(66) Quran, 60:8-9

(67) Quran, 7:179

(68) Quran, 83:13-14

(69) Quran, 2:88

(70) Quran, 2:6-7

(71) Quran, 2:187

(72) Quran, 2:223

(73) Quran, 35:1

(74) Quran, 4:76

(75) Quran, 1:2-3

(76) Quran, 20:74

(77) Quran, 3:110

(78) Quran, 3:110

(79) Quran, 16:43 / 21:7 / 12:109

(80) Quran, 9:5

(81) Quran, 9:1-7

(82) Quran, 4:3

(83) Quran, 16:125

(84) Quran, 2:256

(85) Quran, 19:27-28

(86) The book of Luke, 3:23

(87) The book of Matthew, 1:1

(88) The book of Luke, 1:5

(89) Quran, 10:36

(90) Quran, 7:146

(91) Quran, 34:34-37

(92) Quran, 23:53-56

(93) Quran, 89:15-16

(94) Quran, 6:116

(95) Quran, 10:35-36

(96) Quran, 14:10

(97) Quran, 43:23

(98) Quran, 7:28

(99) Quran, 39:3

(100) Quran, 10:18

(101) Quran, 33:66-68

(102) Quran, 3:79

(103) Quran, 3:191 / 4:82

(104) Quran, 25:43-44

(105) Quran, 7:32

(106) Quran, 42:30

(107) Quran, 57:22-23

(108) Quran, 7:42

(109) Quran, 42:30

(110) Quran, 6:42

(111) Quran, 2:155

(112) Quran, 2:164

(113) Quran, 39:29

(114) Quran, 51:56

(115) Hadith: Tirmidhi

(116) Quran, 76:1

(117) Quran, 67:2

(118) Quran, 3:185

(119) Quran, 29:57

(120) Quran, 23:100

(121) Quran, 77:7-10

(122) Quran, 29:57

(123) Quran, 23:101

(124) Quran, 17:52

(125) Quran, 70:43-44

(126) Quran, 10:45

(127) Quran, 1:4

(128) Quran, 3:185

(129) Quran, 17:13-14

(130) Quran, 99:7-8

(131) Quran, 36:65

(132) Quran, 41:19-23

(133) Quran, 23:102-103

(134) Quran, 43:67

(135) Quran, 75:22-25

(136) Quran, 83:15

(137) Quran, 67:6

(138) Quran, 4:56

(139) Quran, 18:29

(140) Quran, 22:19-22

(141) Quran, 37:64-67

(142) Quran, 47:15

(143) Quran, 40:70-76

(144) Quran, 78:21-28

(145) Quran, 39:16

(146) Quran, 3:185

(147) Quran, 18:107-108

(148) Quran, 18:31

(149) Quran, 36:55-58

(150) Quran, 44:52-56

(151) Quran, 47:15

(152) Quran, 76:13-22

(153) Quran, 43:73

(154) Quran, 78:31-35

(155) Quran, 2:25

(156) Quran, 43:69-72

(157) Quran, 49:13

(158) Quran, 39:6

(159) Quran, 4:1

(160) Qur'an, 6:98

(161) Quran, 35:11

(162) Quran, 40:67

(163) Quran, 22:5

(164) Quran, 95:1-4

(165) Quran, 40:64

(166) Quran, 82:6-8

(167) Quran, 51:56

(168) Quran, 17:62-70

(169) Quran, 2:33)

(170) Quran, 32:18-20

(171) Quran, 59:20

(172) Quran, 28:60-61

(173) Quran, 4:95-96

(174) Quran, 9:19-20

(175) Quran, 57:10

(176) Quran, 16:75-76

(177) Quran, 39:8-9

(178) Quran, 40:58-59

(179) Quran, 11:18-24

(180) Quran, 13:16

(181) Quran, 6:48-50

(182) Quran, 35:19-22

(183) Quran, 39:21-22

(184) Quran, 58:11

(185) Quran, 49:13

(186) Quran, 43:31-32

(187) Quran, 25:20

(188) Quran, 4:32

(189) Quran, 16:93

(190) Quran, 42:13

(191) Quran, 4:17-18

(192) Quran, 2:153

(193) Quran, 2:45

(194) Quran, 7:56

(195) Quran, 9:51

(196) Quran, 8:49

(197) Hadith: Tirmidhi

(198) Hadith: Tirmidhi / Ibn Majah

(199) Quran, 2:272

(200) Quran, 25:67

(201) Quran, 17:26

(202) Quran, 2:152

(203) Quran, 7:56

(204) Quran, 16:91

(205) Quran, 5:89

Note: The Quranic translations of Abdullah Yusuf Ali, M.H.Shakir, Dr.Muhammad Taqi-ud-Din Al-Hilali, Dr. Muhammad Muhsin Khan are used in this book.

www.ingramcontent.com/pod-product-compliance
Lightning Source LLC
Chambersburg PA
CBHW072202090426
42740CB00012B/2350